Doormats and Control Freaks

Doormats and Control Freaks

How to Recognize, Heal
or End Codependent Relationships

Rebekah Lewis

New Horizon Press
Far Hills, New Jersey

New Horizon Press
P.O. Box 669
Far Hills, NJ 07931

Rebekah Lewis
Doormats and Control Freaks: How to Recognize, Heal or End Codependent Relationships

Cover Design: Robert Aulicino
Interior Design: Susan M. Sanderson

Library of Congress Control Number: 2004118080

ISBN: 0-88282-257-8
New Horizon Press

Printed in Canada

2009   2008   2007   2006   2005   /   5   4   3   2   1

Table of Contents

To my boys: The world is yours; take it! I love you.

To my mom, because I know you said the same thing to me that I say to my boys, even when I didn't listen. You've done a wonderful job.

To my family: Mom, Dad, Grandma and my favorite aunt and uncle, for getting me this far in life unharmed, happy and sane. Without you, I'd be lost.

To JJ, you are one in a million. Thanks for everything.

Author's Note

This book accurately conveys the themes central to codependency and control issues and is based upon my research, professional and personal experience. However, the individuals mentioned in this book are not specific individuals but composites and all names are fictitious. For the purpose of simplifying usage, the pronouns *he* and *she* are sometimes used interchangeably.

Introduction
Loving Too Much

A "no" uttered from deepest conviction is better and
greater than a "yes" merely uttered to please,
or what is worse, to avoid trouble.
-Mahatma Gandhi

As a young girl, I knew nothing of hot-button terms like codependency or relationship addiction. What I did know from reading fairy tales was that when Cinderella got dolled up, she hooked herself a prince. The ugly stepsisters—the one with warts and a crooked nose and the one who was rather "fluffy"—were passed over in haste to get to Little Ms. Tiny Feet. Snow White would have died if some young hunk of a man hadn't happened along with the next best thing to CPR... a kiss! And Rapunzel should thank the Lord that a perfectly chiseled hunk knew immediately what to do with her golden hair. Imagine the agony of him climbing her hair for ten stories. I'll bet he was heavy with all those massive muscles. But she took it, all to be saved and live happily ever after.

It never occurred to me that Cinderella could have opened her own successful cleaning business, told that stepmother to kiss her butt and THEN found a man, on her own terms. Snow White could have whipped out her cell phone and dialed 911 before she passed out, summoning a paramedic who'd hold her to nothing except a bill, instead of a lifetime of servitude. And who needs fifty-foot hair? Except to please men who love fifty-foot hair. Golden hair to be exact. Such luxurious strands would have woven into an exceptional ladder had she lopped it off, not to mention leaving Rapunzel with a gorgeous pert bob.

Please don't think that women are the only ones hooked by fairy tale myths. How was it that the Beast just happened to be saved and transformed when Beauty loved him? I wonder what would have happened if Cinderella's hump-backed, mole-faced sister had shown up instead? And all these toad princes? They could join the union, rise up against the machine. Why on earth don't they hack into the wicked witch's spell book to reverse the charm, rather than wasting away on a toadstool, peering through the brush at passing princesses, only to be bound forever to the one who was lonely enough to kiss one? She couldn't be that great if she's going around kissing toads, now could she? Sadly, though, according to some, being in a bad relationship is better than being alone. This becomes the staple of relationship addiction, low self-esteem and codependency.

These simple tales and family dynamics we absorb in childhood set the stage for unhealthy visions of ourselves and our actions and reactions in future relationships. There is a constant debate in psychology: Nature or Nurture? Is it genetics? Our parents? That darn rap music? Who screwed up the children? Much like the chicken and the egg quandary, it may never be solved. Familial relationships, substance abuse and addictions, modern media outlets, gender bias and stereotypes, and the ever growing popularity of dating on the Internet: there are so many factors involved in creating the role of codependent, especially in women. According to Peter Vesgo, President of Health Communications, Inc., 85 percent of the codependency market is female. I was one of them. Men and women, mostly the latter, have strong needs to please others, the need to fit in at all costs. Many insecure people put up with so much to get that modicum of approval we are looking for instead of finding approval within ourselves. The insecure often attract and are attracted by controlling individuals. We will learn why and how these opposites attract each other, practice unhealthy behaviors and sabotage their intimacy again and again. The reasons are many.

It is my hope that we can explore together where codependency originates, how it is perpetuated and the proven twelve-step program I will offer of confidence-boosting techniques, simple strategies and tips to change the boundaries, heal or leave poisonous relationships. By managing this personality disorder I believe we can together take the positive steps needed to conquer it.

Part
◀ 1 ▶

Pleasing Everyone
except Yourself

◀ 1 ▶

The Origins of Codependency: The Loss of Choice and Power

Hannah tells this story of codependency: "I came home from work Tuesday night to a note. 'I know you want things to work out. But I must force myself to move on. You drain me, trying to make everything work for you; you can't make everything perfect.' My codependency has once again destroyed a relationship. Todd has left town for a few days to think. No call yet. I feel almost paralyzed. How did I get this way, and how do I stop?"

What is codependency?

According to Robert Subby, author of *Lost in the Shuffle: A Codependent Reality*, codependency is "an emotional, psychological, and behavioral condition that develops as a result of an individual's prolonged exposure to, and practice of, a set of oppressive rules—rules which prevent the open expression of feelings as well as the direct discussion of personal and interpersonal problems."

The National Mental Health Association defines codependency as "a learned behavior that can be passed down from one generation to another. It is an emotional and behavioral condition that affects an individual's ability to have a healthy, mutually satisfying relationship. It is also known as 'relationship addiction' because people with Codependency often form or maintain relationships that are one-sided, emotionally destructive and/or abusive. The disorder was first identified about ten years ago as the result of years of studying interpersonal

3

relationships in families of alcoholics. Co-dependent behavior is learned by watching and imitating other family members who display this type of behavior."

"Codependency is a set of maladaptive, compulsive behaviors learned by family members in order to survive in a family which is experiencing great emotional pain and stress."[1]

Though there are hundreds of definitions of codependency, the consensus is that it's a learned behavior. What is learned can be unlearned. Like any addiction, it's a long, hard road. However, with proper motivation and lifelines, success is within reach. And, like any addiction, there are obstacles and downfalls out there. Friends, relatives and loved ones, people who are dealing with their own demons may not be prepared to put forth enough effort into helping you cope with yours. You must be your own best advocate. This is a lesson Gail learned the hard way:

"I met my ex-husband halfway between his home and mine so that our daughter could spend a week with him. First of all, we didn't meet at the actual halfway point, we never do. He pleads and cajoles me into driving further; he doesn't have gas money, has to be at work, and has car problems, time constraints, always something. And I always give in, because I don't like confrontation. So I put the extra miles on my car again, exhausted from driving by the time I get there.

"When I see him, he's got a terrible scar across his cheek. It is puffy and red, and mars his good looks. He immediately tells me that he got the cut from falling on the steps in the dark when going into his house. What he doesn't know is that his girlfriend called me the night she put him in rehab (his third trip) and told me that in a drunken rage, he put his head through a window. Familiar territory, his anger. Terrible memories. I know this, but I let him lie and let him believe his lie, let him believe I believe him, as usual. He was always full of stories and dreams and plans that never came to fruition. He's told so many lies and stories that he doesn't know what's true and what's not.

"I don't want to leave my child with him, but I don't want to take away the only thing he has. He's quit his job, every job since I left him, as a matter of fact. He begs me to stay and eat lunch with him, and I want to. I want to stay because I still love him, and I want to make everything all better for him. I want to fix everything. But I know I can't fix him, I can only fix me. And try to bring my child up better, accentuate the positive genes she's received from both of us. I say no, and cry all the way home. I do this every time I drop my daughter off. I feel so guilty; is it my fault he quit his fifteen-year career as an accountant after I left? That he went to jail after assaulting a building? That he's been in and out of the hospital with physical and mental ailments? That he can't keep a job now, or a home, or his finances? If I just… if I just what? If I just tried one more time? I held everything together while we were married. I kept him somewhat sane during his booze battle, but when I couldn't take it anymore, and decided to get my child and myself out, he lost whatever sanity he was holding on to. He wasn't an awful person; he loved us and still does. He was a wonderful provider who wanted the best for his family, but his demons felled his good intentions.

"I can't stop blaming myself, feeling guilty for his decline. I know it's not my fault, I do, but I still wonder. He was self-destructive long before I met him, but I was young and wanted to save him. In fact, I've wanted to save every man in my life. It's a daily struggle not to go back to him. I know he'd stop drinking for a while, I know I could get him working again, saving up his money. I could make him happy again. He loves us and wants his family back. But at the expense of my happiness and our daughter's. This hurts so badly, watching him hurt, and this is why I'm codependent. His pain hurts me worse than my own. After all the damage he's done my daughter and me, I want him to be happy more than I want me to be happy."

One characteristic of codependency is a pervasive feeling of guilt. Guilt for your shortcomings, others' shortcomings, everyone's problems, anything and everything that goes on around you. In codependency, everything can be twisted into your fault, and if it's not your fault in any way possible, you still feel guilty that you can't do anything to fix the problem. Most of the stories I've collected involve guilt. Even when being beaten down physically and verbally, most codependents will find some way to self-blame and this enables the abusers to continue the cycle.

How did we become this way? For the most part, dysfunctional homes breed children, and later adults, with various dependencies. Constant suffering from fear, anger, pain or shame that is ignored or denied is the hallmark of a dysfunctional family. Often there is addiction by family members or close friends to drugs, alcohol, relationships, work, food, sex or gambling, leading to some sort of abuse: physical, emotional or sexual. Dysfunctional families have difficulty with communication and often deny that problems exist. As a result, members of dysfunctional families do not learn appropriate ways to express emotions. Instead they ignore and repress strong feelings.[2] In order to do this, they develop defense mechanisms: denial, detachment and avoidance of emotions necessary to survive. In addition to the extreme tension in the home, attention and energy is increasingly focused on the member with the addiction, with the children and other family members sacrificing themselves, inevitably losing contact with their own needs, desires and sense of self. This, then, is the start of codependency of a new generation.

Many people who grow up in a dysfunctional household become ultraresponsible people not only for themselves, but for the actions and emotions of others as well, especially if they had to take care of parents and siblings. And many of these self-appointed supermen and women concentrate on other people's wants and needs while ignoring their own. They learn to tune out their own desires by "sacrificing" and keeping busy with someone else's issues. The focus is rarely turned inward. In this manner, you fail to acknowledge personal problems. If you can't see it, it must not exist.

But in reality, a codependent may be choking down years of resentment and anger. Many do not know how to say no. You can become known as the "family counselor" to your siblings, spouses and children. But no one even thinks you need his or her help. So you keep on giving and giving, while those around you keep on taking and taking. This is how enabling behavior starts. Then, as this bad habit grows, you actually can create your own monster(s). They have become used to your high level of giving and come to expect it. And they, in turn, become lazier and demand that level of giving.

Sherie told me, "I have working on my codependency issues for YEARS... I thought i had it under control... so much for thinking huh??? I've been with this guy who I thought was soo wonderful for the past four years. Overlooked all his shit Coz... Hey... He didn't HIT me like my EX did... Besides... IM CURED... LOL... what a JOKE!!!! He just left me for his Ex wife... Who is a lesbian... AFTER he beat the shit outta me... And here I sit... Actually WANTING him to come back!! I realized... FINALLY... That CODEPENDENCY is a LIFE LONG recovery and that LEARNED behaviors can take a LIFETIME to UNLEARN!!! For my SANITY I have to learn... Once and for all... What is it that KEEPS me in this cycle... WHY i choose the kind of men I do... And WHAT do I do to change it ONCE AND FOR ALL????"

Overcoming any addiction, including codependency, involves a lifetime struggle. As alcoholics and drug abusers must take it "one day at a time," so must the codependent—or one relationship at a time. Sherie has completed the first step, acknowledging that she has a problem. As I've said before, I'm not preaching from the pulpit; I'm sharing with you my own struggle to leave a situation of codependency. When I took a test for codependency, I was shocked (and yet I knew) how deep I was in the mire. Here is a test for you to take. Please be honest about putting down your replies for only then can we begin walking the path toward independence together. Check those statements that apply to you:

Low Self-Esteem Patterns:
▸ I have difficulty making decisions.
▸ I judge everything I think, say or do harshly, as never "good enough."
▸ I am embarrassed to receive recognition and praise or gifts.
▸ I do not ask others to meet my needs or desires.
▸ I value others' approval of my thinking, feelings and behavior over my own.
▸ I do not perceive myself as a lovable or worthwhile person.

Compliance Patterns:
▶ I compromise my own values and integrity to avoid rejection or others' anger.
▶ I am very sensitive to how others are feeling and feel the same.
▶ I am extremely loyal, remaining in harmful situations too long.
▶ I value others' opinions and feelings more than my own and am afraid to express differing opinions and feelings of my own.
▶ I put aside my own interests and hobbies in order to do what others want.
▶ I accept sex when I want love.

Control Patterns:
▶ I believe most other people are incapable of taking care of themselves.
▶ I attempt to convince others of what they "should" think and how they "truly" feel.
▶ I become resentful when others will not let me help them.
▶ I freely offer others advice and directions without being asked.
▶ I lavish gifts and favors on those I care about.
▶ I use sex to gain approval and acceptance.
▶ I have to be "needed" in order to have a relationship with others.[3]

No one chooses to become codependent. Like Pavlov's dog, certain situations condition certain people to develop codependent tendencies. Just as the dog was slowly trained (inadvertently) to salivate at the signal rather than at the sight or smell of the food, a codependent will naturally react using one of the defense mechanisms listed above. While we are involuntarily trained to act this way, we can choose to change. One of the basic tenets of recovery is that in order to recover we must come face to face with the disease, which is a dysfunctional relationship with the self characterized by living through or for another. Sasha had this problem.

"For a long time I didn't think that I was codependent because I thought you had to be a control freak like most of the women that I observed at Alanon meetings. I thought of myself as someone who lets other people control me so I can please him or her and prevent any kind of confrontation. I guess you could say I am a 'People Pleaser.' After studying codependency some more, I have come to the realization that my actions are kind of controlling in themselves. I control my situation by pleasing everyone and therefore that is comfortable for me no matter how unhealthy, because I am afraid of confrontation."

Some of these basic characteristics are found in homes where abuse, addiction and codependency are prevalent. These constrictions decimate the free and healthy development of an individual's self-esteem and coping skills and lead to unhealthy use of defense mechanisms. People who grow up in families dealing with abuse or addiction may develop a set of unhealthy beliefs and coping mechanisms that can hamper communication skills and emotional development. They may feel uncomfortable or unable to express their feelings openly and may rely on indirect means of communication. They may feel a great deal of pressure to be successful or "perfect." This pressure, combined with a lack of good communication skills, makes it very difficult for such individuals to admit when they are having problems or to ask for help when they need it. As adults, such people may have difficulty forming or maintaining intimate relationships due to the lack of functional role models.[1]

Beyond relationship problems, there are also physical and emotional consequences, such as depression, anxiety, relationship dysfunctions and cycling between hyperactivity and lethargy, as is seen in Bipolar disorders. Gastro-intestinal disturbances, colitis, ulcers, migraine headaches, non-specific rashes and skin problems, high blood pressure, insomnia, sleep disorders and a range of other physical symptoms are evident when codependency is left untreated for a length of time.[4]

Angela relates her own experience of being "trained" for codependency:"I was born into a large family with an alcoholic mother and a father so busy taking care of all of us that we were pretty much left on our own to survive. All of my sibs have experienced problems in relationships and I have one sister severely mentally ill, I think stemming from childhood and a thirty-year abusive relationship with her husband. I dated very little, and then married young to a man who turned out to be so violent that I suffered many, many physical damages; he was also verbally and emotionally abusive. I had two sons by him that I adored. This relationship went on for fourteen years and I could not leave him. When I thought about it, I would become terrified and become even more anxious to please. I knew nothing about codependency, or much about life for that matter. I became so depressed and tired; I was working to pay the bills (he thought his money was his own), taking care of my sons and daughter and doing everything that needed doing. I tried to 'keep the peace' in the family, but then I would get sick of it all and stand up for myself only to find myself with another black eye or broken rib and telling everyone something stupid like I ran into a door, etc., etc., etc. I hated myself for being so weak and did not understand why I could not leave him. Finally, one day he almost injured one of my sons in an attempt to get at me and something in me broke. I kicked him very hard in the shin and then I was beaten to within an inch of my life, literally. I decided to leave him and after three years of him following me and coming into each place I rented and taking over, his parents helped me to get away from him. This was just the beginning; I then went on to have three more abusive marriages, each different from the first, but abusive in different ways.

"My second husband had continual affairs and would take off for days at a time, but I thought all he needed was for someone to really love him and he would be alright. Yeah. The next one got me into drugs and into a lifestyle that was totally out of my ability to cope. The drugs covered the problems, but caused an even worse problem. I was now addicted to a very powerful drug. He was mean, nasty, perverted and totally unfixable. Again, I went into the relationship thinking I could help him by loving him. I was 'rescued' from this relationship by a man who seemed to be a dream come true—romantic, caring, loving and totally in love with me.

However, this man turned out to be the most subtly manipulative person I have ever met. He wanted to control every aspect of my life and for a long time he did. I ended up having a nervous breakdown, then a complete physical breakdown, on a ventilator in the hospital and not expected to live. After that I went to my son and his wife's home in another state to recover.

"While there, my son talked to me about how destructive this man was to me. I began to understand I had a huge problem. Then one day this man had someone else call me pretending to be a credit company. I took the call and it all started up again. The words, I love you and only want you to be happy, I will do anything you want, just come back and we will have a wonderful life. Well, I bought it, to my son's strong disapproval, and went back for a year. It was a year in hell, he and his kids made my life miserable and all the time telling me that I was crazy, I had problems, etc., etc., etc. So, I went into therapy and read some books on codependency and recovery and left him.

"I now live alone and am in therapy and on a lot of medication just to stay stable. I am beginning to understand codependency a little more each day. But, I think back now and realize that I have been in abusive relationships for thirty years, most of my life—what a waste!!! I wish I had found a therapist years ago (I did try, but they just kept prescribing this drug and that drug). I am not happy yet, but I am not sad all the time either. I have to work very hard not to keep telling myself how stupid I was to keep repeating the same mistake over and over. I consider myself a fairly intelligent person, so how could I not have seen what I was doing? I have damaged my own self-esteem more than anyone else could and do not want to keep doing this to myself!!"

Another destructive side effect of codependency is domestic violence. Abuse is not just being hit. Abuse is any action that is harmful or controlling and that affects the well-being of another person. Many people use the term "abuse" to signify physical abuse, but there are many ways of abusing someone besides beating him or her. Physical abuse is the most horrifying and most noticeable of them

all, but it is only one of the many types of abuse. Just as many codependents came from violent homes, the cycle continues, leading
them from one harmful relationship to another. A characteristic of
codependency is the inability to leave a chronically abusive relationship behind, as well as to continue seeking out similar poisonous
relationships. The significant other insists on complete control and
when the need is not met, abuse occurs.

Here are statistics on domestic abuse in the United States:

▶ 60 percent of marriages have some instance of domestic
violence.
National Crime Statistics Report

▶ Women account for 95 percent of all victims of domestic
violence.
*Bureau of Justice Statistics Special Report, U.S.
Department of Justice*

▶ The single largest cause of injury to women is domestic
violence.
*First Comprehensive National Health Study of American
Women, the Commonwealth Fund*

▶ A woman is physically abused in the U.S. every nine sec-
onds.
Family Violence Prevention Fund

▶ Spousal murder and murder by acquaintances account for
50 percent of all women murdered in the U.S.
Journal of Trauma

▶ Emergency Department records indicate that as few as 5
percent of domestic violence victims are actually identified
as such.
American Journal of Public Health

▶ Domestic violence begins early: between 25 and 30 percent of adolescent relationships are abusive in some way.
   L.A. Commission on Assaults against Women

▶ In 90 percent of domestic violence cases involving battered women, the abuse took place in the presence of children.
   National Crime Statistics Report

In Clinton Clark's *I'm Not OK When...You're Not*, the author details many ways in which an abuser can exert control. Among them are violence and rage, coercion, the deliberate use of words or actions to belittle or shame, unreasonable expectations, false affection, offering of emotional or material "rewards" and invasion or denial of privacy.[5]

Remember, physical abuse is not the only way a codependent is controlled. Mental anguish pains much more than bodily injury at times and is much more effective at times. Some people have cultivated the ability to control others with minimal remarks or gestures; they, in effect, find that proverbial button and play with it as they please. As Clark asserts, "It's important to acknowledge that all destructive control behaviors attack self esteem and cause decay or an erosion of self worth."[5]

Our goal is to admit the codependency characteristics that we have, take stock of all the positives and negatives in our lives, and work from there on recovering, healing and starting fresh. Whether you're sixteen or sixty, it's not too late.

◀ 2 ▶

Recollections of Childhood Dysfunction: How I Became a Doormat

Relationship addiction started early in my life. Once I complained to an older woman I knew that a group of ugly men were whistling at me as I walked by. She said, "When the ugly ones DON'T whistle, that's when you have something to worry yourself about." Ever since then, if I don't get a look or a whistle, I wonder what's wrong with me.

After observing my role models in the media, television and movies, I was ripe for codependency. I had a crush a day, fell in and out of love as often as I changed clothes. I needed boys' attention constantly. If they weren't looking, I was doing something wrong: skirts too low, necklines too high. I'd fix the problem and try again. Any attention was good; I didn't care if it was for the wrong reasons. As long as the boys took notice. One of them was Alex. He was über gorgeous and rich beyond my wildest dreams. He lived in a very wealthy neighborhood, the type where Madonna and Shaq live now. He was in my math class and was a senior when I was a freshman. When he started talking to me, I thought I was dreaming. I would have done anything to keep his attention. Though I was a good student in math, I managed to dumb myself down enough to pull an F, all to have an excuse to talk to Alex, to ask him questions, to be tutored. I hoped by making him feel smart and "manly," he'd want to spend more time with me. I was always on, flirting and showing as much skin as accidentally as possible. If Alex was looking, I was performing. Up until that point, I hadn't had many dates. I'd gone on group outings with friends, had kissed a few boys, but that was about it. I'd done no heavy petting and was fairly inexperienced, but I knew there was much more out there. What I didn't realize at that time was that I would often mistake lust for genuine personal interest and affection.

About a block away from my high school was Jennifer's apartment and every day at lunch, a group of us would walk over there to eat and watch soap operas. My friends and I were fairly innocuous, sitting around chatting till it was time to go back to class. Until Alex.

I spent so much time trying to get his attention that when he asked to come to lunch with us, I was overjoyed. He and a few of his friends came with us to Jennifer's. He and I sat on the couch and began making out. He started to move farther than I was prepared for, but I wanted so much for him to like me, that I let him continue. (*I wanted so much for him to like me...* that thought would pervade my life... my worst personality trait.) Eventually I let him separate me from my friends and he forced me to go much further than I was prepared for. At first, I went along with it, desperately hoping that it would make him fall in love with me and we'd be rich and happy forever and ever. When he became more forceful I resisted, but in the end I wasn't strong enough to stand up for myself and insist that he respect my limits. He forced me to perform oral sex on him. He knew that he could use me and he did, later taking pleasure in humiliating me in front of his friends.

That wasn't the end of it. Every day after that in our math class he sat behind me, calling me a slut and throwing things at me, passing notes around about the things I'd done, and things I hadn't. He told everyone around the school that I'd slept with him and all his friends and done things I'd never heard of. Instead of standing up for myself, telling him off, kicking his ass, telling the truth, I let it happen. I thought it was my fault in some way—skirt too high, shirt too low. I thought I'd never have a boyfriend again and that's what I was worried about. Not my dignity or my pride, just whether I was still datable.

Soon after that, I moved to another state. I started fresh, with a clean slate. It was my perfect opportunity to change and become a stronger person. Instead, I only progressed further in my role as a needy, budding codependent.

I kept dating, going farther and farther with the boys. In my sophomore year I had my eye on a senior named Peter. Remembering, I wish I could ground me, shake me, wake me up... do something! Probably you can see it in me, but it's so hard to see it in ourselves— this rut I was in, this pattern of self-abuse. Peter was in the popular crowd; I was not. I had a few friends, but I wasn't outgoing enough to be in that group. I was cute, had a nice curvy body, but I wasn't the blonde bombshell Cinderella was. He was a blonde Adonis, gorgeous... rich. Being attracted to guys like him had become a pattern for me. Peter was hot pickings. I couldn't seem to get him... he wasn't as easy to string along as all the other guys were; he didn't even seem to notice me. I sent the requisite secret admirer letters, left excellent clues so that if he wanted to find me he could. He went through girlfriend after girlfriend without taking the slightest interest in me, which, of course, made me want him so much more. We had no classes together, but I'd catch his eye walking down the hall a few times a day. He'd smile, I'd smile and that was the extent of it.

By some quirk of fate, the last two weeks of the year, he was switched into my study hall class. I was floored and I knew this was the "in" I needed. He couldn't resist me. He winked at me when he walked in and sat right next to me. I showed a little leg and a lot of boobs and got the attention I needed. We immediately started passing silly love notes and whispering in the back of the room. We talked after class and the next day he gave me a ride home from school. Every day that week, he took me home. I was in love, true love... I knew it had to be the end all-be all love of my life. We talked on the phone till late in the night and he played love songs for me. Every time I hear "Wild Horses" by the Stones, I remember Peter. Not fondly, either.

The last week of school, we got even closer. He took me to a park down the street from our school every day at lunch and after school, and we went in and made out. I wouldn't let him go any further, but I knew that I would say yes to him, if and when he asked, give him what I hadn't given anyone else. He had been interested in me longer than any other boy had, so I supposed I owed him. I wanted to keep him and would do anything to achieve that goal.

At this point I wasn't allowed to date. I wasn't allowed to wear makeup and I wasn't allowed to talk on the phone to boys. I had to talk in the closet late at night... and often I was caught and grounded. So when Peter asked me on my first real date, I wondered if I would even be allowed to go. I got lucky, but forever wished I hadn't. He wanted to take me out for a birthday dinner. The morning of my sixteenth birthday, I remember my mom making me a cake and playing "Sixteen Candles" for me. Now that I was sixteen, my mother decided that I was old enough to be allowed to date and gave me permission to go. I called Peter and told him the good news, and he said he'd pick me up at seven for dinner and a movie. My first real date!

At seven, Peter showed up at my doorstep. He was my white knight. He was wearing a suit and a tie, and came in, conversed with my mother and her husband like a true gentleman. He told them of his plans for me... dinner at a ritzy restaurant that I'd never been to, and then on to a play in the city. *Cats* was showing and I felt like a real lady. I was swirling above the clouds and I couldn't stop smiling. I'd found the man of my dreams and I'd never look for another.

We left my house and Peter said that he had to stop back by his house to pick up something. I said no problem; I wasn't about to disagree with anything he said. He had complete control over me. We pulled up to his house and he invited me in. He said his parents were out of town and he had to make sure the animals were fed. I thought, *How sweet... he loves his animals*. What a fool I was. Peter showed me around the house, ending in his bedroom. We went in there and lay on the bed, kissing, him fondling my breasts. I was okay with that; after all, this was the man I was going to marry. Like Jekyll and Hyde, his gropes became rougher then, almost vicious. I cried out that he was hurting me, but he ignored me and continued. It hurt and I had tears in my eyes... not of joy, but of pain now. And fear.

I begged him to stop hurting me; I pleaded. He laughed and said that he knew I liked it that way. The pretty dress I had picked out was pulled this way and that as he tried to get to my bare skin. Finally, it tore down the side and he pulled the whole thing off. I was really crying then and he put all his weight on top of me, his hands around my neck, and told me not to make another sound. I knew what was going to happen, and while I'd told myself this was the man I wanted to have all of me, this wasn't how it was supposed to go down. He forced me to have sex with him.

Afterwards, I was hurt and ashamed. I was also afraid that Peter might beat me up for crying, for making a mess in his room. I did the best I could to clean myself off with his sheet and put my torn dress back on. I was sobbing, thinking of how much potential that day had held.

Peter came back in the room then and told me to get out of his house. I left and got in his car. I wondered if we were still going out... I can't believe I was still so naive. Driving down his street, we passed another car full of girls. Peter slowed to a stop and began to talk to the driver of the other car, a perky blonde cheerleader with huge boobs and a penchant for Peter. Right in front of me, he asked her to meet him in twenty minutes at a local restaurant. He told her he was starved and wanted to get rid of me quickly. I was humiliated so badly, I wanted to hide my face and die. The girls in the car laughed and we drove off.

There was no dinner; I don't think he ever planned to take me anywhere but to his bed. When he pulled up in front of my house, I got out and he squealed off. I knew I couldn't go home... I'd only been gone thirty minutes. My whole life ripped out of me in less than thirty minutes. I walked to the park, wincing with each step. I sat on a swing for two hours and tried to figure out what I'd done wrong. How did I mess that one up? What had I done to make him not love me? What could I have done differently? Today I hate how I was back then. I didn't blame him, I blamed me. He raped me and I thought it was my fault.

Around ten that night I went back home, thankful that I was able to get in without having to talk to anyone. I grabbed my pajamas and jumped in the shower. When I got out, I just wanted to go to bed and cry myself to sleep. I must have done something wrong; why did Peter like the other girl and not me? What made her worthy of dinner and made me worthy of rape? What did I do wrong? In my head, I made up a night, the night I would have written for myself. In my story, Peter was the charming prince: he held open doors, pulled out my chair, bought me steak and lobster. He held my hand and attempted only a goodnight kiss. He showered me with compliments and pleasantries. I didn't tell anyone the truth till ten years later, when I cried like it had been that night. I was a woman now and not at all ready for the world of men, not this kind. This was the only kind I'd find for a long while though, but only because that was the kind I looked for.

The first half of my junior year, I was crazy in love every other day. I pushed Alex and Peter to the back of my mind, but they'd left scarred trails in their wakes. I had a string of boyfriends... James, Jason, Aaron, Mark, Richard and so many more. I couldn't keep up with them. I thought if I made the guy feel good, he'd stay with me. No pleasure for me, only for them. I never had sex with them, though. For that I am happy.

I kept my relationships pretty light for a while, until David moved into town. The boys before him were only a drop in the ocean compared to the abuse I suffered by his mouth and hands.

He came to live with his mom halfway through my junior year. We shared one class together—history. Most of the students at the school had wealthy parents and I was paid for by my grandma. I lived on the wrong side of the tracks and hadn't been one of "them" all my life. I had dated most of the boys in that class and that didn't help my approval rating either.

When David walked in the room, I knew he would be "the one." Again. I know, I said that all the time and I believed it every time. David had piercing grey eyes and soft, curly blonde hair. I thought he was gorgeous, my mom hated him: perfect combination. It was the most volatile relationship I've ever had. He was insanely jealous and deeply disturbed. We broke up and made up weekly. He was a virgin and I took his virginity. After that, we had sex everywhere, all the time. He asked me to marry him, even bought me a ring. When it was good, it was very very good. When it was bad... it was a bruiser. He sent me pages and pages of love letters daily and I did the same for him. If he caught me looking at or talking to another guy, he'd scream and berate me and break up with me.

There were only thirty people in my junior class, half of which were guys. I wasn't even allowed to stand next to them or he'd say I didn't love him anymore. I had to move by myself in all of my classes so that I wouldn't be next to any males. I couldn't go to lunch with any groups if guys were involved and I couldn't do anything after hours with my classmates. My mom was so right: I should have stayed away from him.

Once, while riding in his car, I glanced out the window. Who knows what I was looking at, maybe nothing, maybe something. He thought I was looking at a guy in another car and he hit me over the head. This happened quite often; the only thing that changed was the weapon. He alienated me further from my class and my friends when I needed them most. My mom hated him because he was so possessive. He dictated what I wore, where I went. Whenever we had fights, he'd sit behind me in class and throw things at me, write bad notes about me and pass them to his friends. He'd whisper "slut, bitch, tramp," and his friends would giggle and call me names too. The girls hated me too and didn't stand up for me. And just as I did nothing when Alex did this to me, I sat humiliated but silent, willing him to stop. He never did.

That lasted for a year. Through it all, I wanted to marry him. I thought that this was the way relationships were supposed to be. This is what I had witnessed from my only role models. Finally, though, I'd had enough. I was working at a local store at the time and he'd just broken up with me for the umpteenth time. A guy who worked with me asked me out. Paul was tall, strong and pretty handsome, so I said yes. I still didn't realize that type of guy was wrong for me. I'm learning that lesson to this day. We went out a few times and I asked him to a dance.

David showed up in the parking lot with a gun. Paul went home and never spoke to me again. After that, every guy that I dated was either beat up or threatened with worse by David. He said that if he couldn't have me, no one would. I felt that I couldn't tell my mother; I hated to admit she'd been right about him. The only thing that saved me from a lifetime of hell with him was his mother's kicking him out. He had to move out of state after that and I didn't hear from him again for years. Unfortunately, I didn't escape without severe psychological damage.

I met David again by chance about six years ago. I was in my best shape ever and had a better figure than when we were together. My hair was dyed blonde and I had tan, ample breasts from having kids and a tiny waist. He lived in Alexandria and I lived in Shreveport. I went to visit a friend who lived in Mississippi and called David out of the blue. I hadn't spoken to him in ten years.

David and I agreed to meet the next week. He drove down,and when he got out of his jeep, it took my breath away. All those old feelings came rushing back. He was amazed to see me looking so good. Apparently he'd married the girl that he dated after me and she'd ballooned to 200 pounds and treated him very badly. Isn't that what they all say? Anyhow, he made me feel so good about myself, compliments left and right. He spent a good hour apologizing for treating me so terribly when we were young. He lamented that I was "the one" and we should have been the ones who married and that he made the biggest mistake of his life when he let me go.

Shortly after that, we agreed to meet in Montgomery at a diner. Montgomery was halfway between his home and mine. I drove two hours, so excited, thinking this may be a new start for me. We met at the restaurant and the craziest thing happened. I offered myself on a platter and he refused. At the last minute, he didn't want to cheat on his wife. I should have been impressed at what a man he'd become, but I was humiliated. He said some mumbo jumbo about when he got his divorce, he'd call me and I left in tears. A few years later, David's best friend called me up and told me that David couldn't stop think-ing about me. I asked if he was still married and of course, he was. But his friend swore that David talked about me constantly and regretted turning me down that day. He tried to set up a meeting again, but I turned him down. He called and emailed a few times after that, to no avail. I haven't heard from him since. I'll never forget the hell he put me through, and I'm proud that I left that one behind.

Looking back, I should have learned from those bad relation-ships, but it would still be fifteen years before I stepped completely out of myself, observed, hated what I saw and did something about it. The good news is I did.

If you've been part of codependent relationships you too can change. I did a complete overhaul. For myself. You can too.

◀ 3 ▶

Learning by Mistakes:
Stories from between
a Rock and a Hard Place

Knowing you're not alone is sometimes the best medicine of all; this is why meetings and self-help groups can provide insights we need for eventual change. We want to share our story, yes, but we also want to know that someone else out there has screwed up too. We like to hear how people have gotten themselves into hot water and how they got out. We nod our heads and feel the pain, because we've been through it too. As they tell about relapses, we understand, because winning over our demons is the hardest thing we've had to do. We are brimming with advice for them—"Leave him!" "He's no good." "She's draining you!" "You deserve better than that."

Changing ourselves, however, is easier said than done. You think like me—I *know* what I need to do to modify my relationship addictions; I *know* what I'm doing wrong; I *know* what types to stay away from. I *know* I'm worth more than I give myself credit for and I deserve the best. I *know*. But my actions never correlate with what I *know*. Cognitive dissonance—struggling to coordinate your beliefs and behavior—rears its ugly head. We want to alter our moods, our clinginess, our need for attention, but in the end it's more painful to be alone. The end product would be worth it if we could just get through the pain of transformation. I tell my boys, as you tell your children, if they work hard in school, it will pay off. Get through the misery of term papers and homework, studying and early nights, and one day they'll have good jobs and whatever they want in life. We tell our children to suffer temporarily for future happiness—why can't we do the same for ourselves?

Throughout this chapter are true accounts of women and men who've been codependents, some in worse situations than I can imagine. In gathering research some stories were written by hand, some emailed, some told in person, but every word is their own and, be forewarned, terrifying and painful to the core. But I know their pain. As do you. In reading these experiences I hope that you'll take from them the knowledge that you are not alone, as well as finding some courses of action to make a change. It is easier to manage other people's lives, especially for codependents. Begin today by starting a notebook where you collect ideas and strategies that you would share with each of the people. Journal these solutions and apply them to your own life. Because while the specifics of our circumstances may vary, our codependence and our need to please others at any cost is what we have in common with each other.

One woman who wrote me had agonizing experiences. She wrote:

"I can't leave him.

"He says the right words but his actions never match up. He blames me for everything and tells me I need to take care of my own problems. He accuses me of lying, cheating, conspiring against him with my friends and family. He argues with me over everything I do. He goes through my personal items. He watches my every movement. He constantly invades my privacy and says that he just wants to be close to me. When things don't go his way he frightens me through confrontations. Three weeks ago he escalated the confrontation to a physical level. He didn't hit me but he came after me. I locked myself in the bathroom with the phone, but he disconnected the phone lines so I couldn't call the police. I asked him to move out and he said he would but he did nothing except pressure me to try to work out the problems. He tries to makes me feel guilty for my decision. I own the house that we live in. I ended up seeing a psychiatrist for the panic attacks and anxiety I was suffering as a result of this relationship. He put me on anti-depressants when I told him that part of my anxiety was the realization that I put myself in this position and did not seem to have an easy way out. He told me to get out of the house whether or not it was mine and be safe. When I went home my boyfriend tried to pretend that everything was okay, that we would be able to work through our problems. Whenever I made a suggestion about helping him find his own place he became angry so I backed off.

"One night I left while he was gone and stayed at my mother's. I asked for her help, which was very difficult for me, and she said that if he was still at my house the next day (he had been promising to leave and go to a hotel until he got a place) that she would confront him. I asked if she was afraid of him and she said 'absolutely not.' She pointed out to me that he is intimidated by her because she is not afraid of him. He is intimidated by anyone who confronts him and is not afraid. My mother was right, I am afraid and that gives him the power to intimidate me. She talked to him, she gave him money, she helped him pack and she moved him out to a motel the next day. The fact that he cooperated so easily amazed me. He even gave my mother a hug and thanked her for the support and help. I was stunned.

"Since he moved out I have been babysitting his son while he works at night because he does not have anyone to watch him and because I did not want the child to suffer through this transition. He has begun to use his son as a way of making me interact with him. I have told him I cannot talk to him but when he brings his son to my house, he stands at the door saying he needs to talk to me and then engages me in an emotional argument about our relationship. He calls me in the middle of the night using the excuse that his son is here and then tries to draw me into an argument. One night I was determined not to take any more; I shut the front door in his face and locked it. He started pounding on my bedroom window, which I tried to ignore. He went back to the front door and started yelling, 'I want to talk to my son!' His son went outside for a few minutes, then came back in and his father finally left.

"I have never been this afraid of someone. He is intimidated by everyone around me, won't even come near the house if he sees another person's car in the driveway. Everyone says that I need to let go of my fear. Why can't I do that? Thank God I have come to terms with many, many things and am over him. When I was ready to speak to him again, I listened and I talked and I put in my licks in a gentle way. He swore it was over, that he was going to AA and would never cheat on me again. He admitted he was at the bottom and that he wanted to be well. I sent him some gentle emails about how much I understood him and what he was doing to himself. It was all his choice, but I told him that if he broke the promises he had made to himself, and to me, that I would wash my hands of him entirely. I took a stroll over to the meeting place to see if his car was at the AA meeting. It was. He emailed me after the meeting and thanked me for my emotional support. He told me how much he needed to hear what I had to say and that he was trying to straighten out his life.

"Since that time, I have been very busy working. I have thought about him on occasion, but not with rancor. He called me recently to tell me how he was doing. He was crying over another woman. Nothing had changed at all. I was very happy and proud of myself that I was able to say to him, 'You are using me at your convenience—all over again. Don't ever call back. God did not put me on this earth to cater to you, to fix the unfixable, so you're on your own—fix yourself. I won't let the positive things in my life be contaminated by your problems.' And I meant it, finally."

As I said in the beginning of this book, women more predominantly take the doormat role in relationships, but men can also be sucked into playing a part. Brian is a man who is struggling with this role. He has noticed that women who have been "hurt" seem to be attracted to him. Often, he feels that he becomes their "safe harbor." Usually he does not mind lending his support, but occasionally he has gotten hurt in the process:

"Once I met a married woman who was obviously very unhappy about something, so I asked what was wrong. She proceeded to tell me all about how lousy her marriage was, how her husband was cheating on her... So I told her she deserved better, and that she needed to be strong and stand up for herself, even if it meant leaving him. She brightened up and thanked me as she went home. Our whole conversation lasted about an hour. The following week the same woman approached me saying she had left her husband for good. She continued to say I had inspired her to leave and she didn't think she had the courage to do it alone, so I told her I would stand beside her the entire time, which I did. (She still hasn't gotten divorced, I doubt she will.) Unfortunately, we got far too close, far too quickly. I figured that I was not the one having problems, that I would just be there for her and be supportive, and if this led to something more, so be it. It did. She began to talk about changing her mind. She seemed reluctant to go through with the divorce. I told her, in many different ways, that I didn't think it would be a good idea to remain in the marriage. I reminded her that she told me in the beginning she wanted me to keep her from losing her resolve, but she wouldn't accept that I really was interested in her well-being. She has all the signs of a codependent, and it seems like I am one as well. I'm supportive, but frequently the women I have relationships with just don't appreciate it. I've decided not to let this happen again, but how can I stop being codependent? Stop being such an enabler?"

Sharlize is beginning to realize how she became codependent:

"My father was an alcoholic and I have always feared confrontation. Now I am having the same problems with my boyfriend. I know he is not good for me yet I NEED HIM TO NEED ME. Though, when I talk to him and he wants to get back into the relationship, I know he is not the one for me. Sometimes I still feel very close to him and when he is not yelling at me or belittling me I am fine. But I never know when his next blow-up will be. WHY DO I ALLOW MYSELF TO ACCEPT THIS BEHAVIOR AND CRAVE HIS ATTENTION?"

Another man, Stan, has recently begun to realize how badly he needs some help:

"Lately I have been doing some research, and I have come to believe I am codependent. I recently began seeking professional help and hope to start getting counseling soon. My last relationship was with a woman who is mentally ill. In the course of our breakup, I

finally began to recognize certain patterns in my life. I always seem
to find myself in relationships with someone who is in the midst of
a crisis. Whether I am attracted to such people, or they are attracted
to me, I don't know. I wish I could say I'm just chivalrous and want
to help people, but that's not really it. I've already had one failed
marriage, as well a string of disastrous relationships. I'm sure I must
have spotted some of these patterns long before now, but I'm just
beginning to understand that the source of the problem lies in me.
I've read something recently that seems to apply to me: I do the
wrong things for the right reasons. I'm very lonely and sad at times,
but I haven't lost my faith yet. And I'm really looking forward to
finally taking some steps to improve. I think that I may be a codependent, but I also feel that I am a strong person. This is confusing
and hard to accept at times, because I do not know how to associ-
ate a personality that is 'strong willed' with one that is 'codependent.' I guess the reason I think I'm codependent is because many of
my past relationships, including my marriage, were very destructive
emotionally to both me and my respective significant others. I
remained with one woman for seven months because she had problems with her parents divorcing and I wanted to be there for her
when she needed me. That was while I was still in high school. When
I went to college the relationship didn't work anymore, so we drifted
apart.

   "About a month into my first semester of college, I met another
girl who had numerous personal problems and soon I found that she
was clinging to me. I felt that I could help her socially, academically
and emotionally if I remained with her. In the end, however, she just
'used' me physically for about nine months and drained me emotionally. I thought I was helping her problems. Finally, I became dis-
gusted with the way the relationship was turning out and abruptly
decided not to see her anymore.

   "Three months after I separated myself from that emotionally
draining situation, I began another relationship with a woman who
was having problems with her family and her personal identity. I
remained in that relationship for over two years and finally ended it
just a few weeks ago. In each of these cases, I believe that I entered
into an intimate relationship with these women in order to help

them or save them. I never considered myself when starting these relationships.

"I now feel drained of emotion and extremely reluctant to enter another relationship with anyone for a very long time. Or rather, at least until I know exactly what I want for myself and until I find someone who knows and understands my needs and who can take care of herself."

Melanie is another individual with a poignant story about struggling with codependency. A recovering drug addict, Melanie spent thirteen years in Narcotics Anonymous. Now she has come to believe that she was addicted not only to drugs, but to relationships as well. Over the years, she has come to recognize a pattern in her life in which her drug use corresponded to her feelings of low self-esteem when a relationship didn't work out. Although she was able to gain control over her drug addiction, she still found herself involved in relationships in which she was used emotionally, physically and financially. She told me that she submitted to this because "I didn't think I could keep a relationship without allowing it to happen." It took Melanie a long time to recognize that all of the people who used her discarded her once they had gotten what they wanted from her. Every time she was rejected in this way, she would begin a downward spiral of depression and drug abuse, which she describes as, "you hurt me so I'll hurt me too."

Even after years of drug-free living, Melanie still hadn't gained the emotional strength to resist harmful relationships. One day while she was attending a meeting at a local treatment center, she ran into a man she had known and been attracted to in the past. When she saw him again, the attraction returned immediately. Unfortunately, this man was an alcoholic, unemployed, with expensive habits and a violent temper. According to Melanie, he was also controlling, manipulative and a thief. After they had been dating for a short time, Melanie allowed him to move in with her and soon she began to notice things that were missing. She even describes going to the local pawnshop to buy back her own possessions. Her boyfriends got a DUI driving her car and Melanie was the one who had to pay to get it out of impound. Worst of all, his constant use of drugs and alcohol and his constant nagging and criticizing eventually prompted Melanie to begin using with him, destroying her "clean time," an achievement of which she had been very proud. Once she began to drink and use drugs again, her partner assumed the dominant role in the relationship and gained complete control once he successfully separated her from friends and family who disapproved of her habits.

The breaking point for Melanie came when her employer went bankrupt and she lost her job. Her partner, who was unemployed, had run up a large debt on her behalf and she had no way of paying it. When she decided to file for bankruptcy, he left her. As Melanie says, "It was as if I was a lottery ticket, and now that I'd paid off, he didn't need me anymore, so on to the next scratch-off." Despite feeling used, Melanie admits that she was glad to see this man go. She had become frightened by his threats and violent behavior, which extended to her family as well as herself.

Although she recognizes the destructive patterns of her behavior and attitudes, Melanie is still having trouble bringing about real change in her life. She is aware that she put up with lousy treatment in the past just to avoid being alone, but she also admits that she is currently dating a new man, a drug addict who is unreliable at work and persuades her to slack off as well. Melanie went back to college after losing her job and already she sees the negative effects this man is having on her life, as she is missing classes, faltering academically, and beginning to have financial difficulties again. During a recent period that her boyfriend spent in the hospital, Melanie came to realize how damaging this relationship has been, and she is once again striving to reverse the negative patterns in her life. Yet she worries about her ability to maintain an independent attitude and lifestyle without falling prey to controlling partners. As she says herself, "Again and again, I allow them control, knowing full well they'll destroy everything I've accomplished prior to meeting them. But I simply can't stop."

Shane has been separated from his wife for almost two years and has begun to realize that he seems to be extremely codependent to the point of being addicted to her:

"I am currently in recovery. I go to several AA meetings a week. My wife and I have had an ongoing pattern of coming together for several weeks of great happiness and contentment, followed by a period of her pulling away from me to the point she ends up, 'not knowing if she wants to be married to me.' We have gone through this cycle about six times in the past two years. We only have sex a few times a year and I'm so lonely I can't stand it. I have made many attempts to be social, but I find that on my own it's very hard for me. I attempted suicide twice in the past two years, almost succeeding the second time. Immediately after the last attempt, I ended up in the hospital with severe heart problems that nearly killed me. As a result, I'm hardly able to work and am having difficulty supporting myself. I just started a job a week ago delivering fast food in the evenings but the hours and physical work are killing me.

"My wife and I opened our own restaurant several years ago and it has been very successful. She has effectively, over the past two years, excluded me from the business and finances. Everything we had was in her name and she is making every attempt to cut me out. After my suicide attempt and heart problems last year, she told me that she wanted a divorce. She wanted to avoid having to pay any of my medical bills and was afraid that she would get stuck having to take care of me if my health deteriorated any further. At that time I was taking some really strong pain medication for my heart condition and it affected my thoughts and behavior to the point that my whole family was frightened and pulled away from me. I have seen little of any of them since then.

"I feel alone. I feel worthless. I'm exhausted and in pain. My financial situation is really getting desperate, to the point that I am skipping several meals a week because I can't afford to go to the grocery store. I've lost twenty pounds in the past six weeks. When I first met my wife I had a good job with a nice salary, but I put all of my savings into our business. I have nothing left and am afraid that I'm never going to be able to work normally again.

"My wife is back to saying that she doesn't want to be married to me anymore, and this time I think she is serious. The last time I talked to her she was very cold and distant, even angry. I feel like I'm going crazy. I thought she would change her mind about a divorce after a few weeks, like in the past, but this time her behavior is not following the usual pattern. She's not talking about a divorce at the moment, but she seems to think we should give up on our marriage. Lately I've been having suicidal thoughts again and I don't know what to do. I want her back no matter how badly she treats me. I know this is wrong and even pathetic, but I can't help feeling this way. I made an appointment with an attorney yesterday, thinking that getting into a 'fight' mode might help me get out of my depression. However, I don't want to risk making her angry by threatening her (she would take my filing for a divorce as a real threat) in case she changes her mind and decides to come back to me.

"Although I don't want a divorce, I see it as the only way I'm going to get my hands on some money for all of my hard work in our business. My wife is making a good salary and I'm living on nothing. She even bought a house a year ago, with our savings. She's making monthly house payments, has a gardener and a housekeeper, and I'm going hungry. I feel like a divorce is the only way I can get something for myself. I don't know what to do. I go to therapy every week and it's helpful but it's really the only support I'm getting right now. My wife and I still love each other but she's an alcoholic, not willing give up the booze, and she's a terrible workaholic. I've got to make a change or I won't survive."

Kacey is from a dysfunctional family:

"I don't know the roots of the dysfunctions. My mom is a codependent in that she feels vulnerable and trapped in her relationship with my dad, yet she remains anyway. I'm codependent in that I have had two relationships with guys with a variety of problems from dysfunctional families of their own. Both of these men were addicts and had addicts in their families. I had a very hard time getting out of these relationships because I cared for them and didn't want to hurt them. In the meantime I found that I ended up hurting myself instead. I have just moved into a new apartment and although many things need to be fixed I find it hard to stand up for myself. I tell the landlord what bothers me, but then don't hold him to fixing it. I'm trying to figure out if I am justified in trying to get out of the lease. I'm feeling trapped and vulnerable myself. I find that I have difficulty relating to men in authority. This causes me difficulty at work and many conflicts, which I hope to learn to avoid. I have a hard time developing friendships."

Sarah, another codependent, is extremely depressed:

"I have tried anti-depressants but I think I need to fix my problem first. I am living with an alcoholic and the first year of our relationship I drank with him also. Eventually I realized how bad this was for me and made a decision to drink much less. I encouraged my boyfriend to do the same. This never worked for more than two to three weeks at a time. We would always end up fighting about something and he would binge, making me really angry. I kept a lot of anger in me and when I drank I would get physical. Once I stopped drinking with him, we still had arguments, but I was able to handle them better.

"I am angry with a lot of things in this relationship. I am hurt but I love this guy. I can't stay away from him; I still think I can fix all of his problems. He will not respect my standards and the limits that I set. One night he refused to leave after an ugly evening and decided to sleep in the car in my driveway. I kept telling him to get out of my driveway, which led to him getting angry and forcing his way into the house. The confrontation soon escalated to a physical level and I hit him in the head. I was so angry. Today I am embarrassed and ashamed that I acted that way but realize I needed help. He provoked me, I responded and then he called 911, which only made things worse between us. Will this ever get better?

"I can see this is never going to end. I can't make him better but I can't leave."

As I gathered these stories I felt deep sorrow. I feel the need to wipe their tears away and ease all the pain. I know I can't fix their problems. I have learned that only the codependent person can fix his or her disease. I can only be a sounding board, a person with a little wisdom, some advice and a lot of experience. Part of codependency is wanting to make everyone better and neglecting yourself.

I've come to realize that the only way to recover is to learn how to be selfish and to put yourself first. Doing that without guilt has been a consistent problem in most of the accounts I've received. However, as you read these stories as well as others throughout this book, look into yourself. Do you recognize some of their experiences, thoughts and pain as similar to your own? I know I do. This recognition is necessary if you are to take the first step to curing your disease. Insight, then action is the plan.

◀ 4 ▶

Don't Be the Glue
That Holds Another's Pieces Together

Are you an enabler? Answer each of the following questions as honestly as you can:

1. Have you seen or know your partner sneaks a drink or more alone in the daytime at home?
2. Do you pretend there is another reason for his or her behavior when you know he or she has been drinking?
3. Do you blame yourself and feel his or her drinking is your fault?
4. Do you talk about other things but not you partner's drinking?
5. Do you pay his or her bills or loan money to your partner?
6. Do you drink together because you want to save the relationship?
7. Do you say you'll leave but keep giving your partner who drinks another chance?
8. Do you keep making false excuses to children, bosses and friends about what is wrong with your partner?

If you said yes to all or almost all of these, you win the doormat, most tread-upon rug, award, for certain. As you read other stories about people just like you and me I hope you will feel a little better. I have found they make me stronger; they let me know that I'm not alone. Other people have come through serious codependent situations with family, friends, lovers and enemies. Yet they have become empowered. I hope they give you the same insight and strength that they gave to me. First, though, you must, as they have, develop insight into your problem. Here is one especially affecting story.

Casey, perhaps like you, was addicted to an addict. She has come to believe that she has a disease, which she sees affecting every aspect of her life. At times, she says, she is unable to control her emotions. Sometimes she takes out her negative feelings on friends and family members. Although she has made efforts to detach herself emotionally from the addict in her life, she confesses to having an "uncontrollable compulsion" to do things for him. She gives him money, food and cigarettes. She has loaned him her car, lied for him, paid fines that he incurred and taken over responsibilities for him.

Casey says that she frequently promises herself that she will change her behavior, but when confronted with a situation that requires her to stand up for herself, she crumbles. She feels that she is unreliable and incapable of living a normal life as a codependent. She recognizes that if she allows it, her disease will destroy her other relationships and interfere with her work. Sometimes she has short periods of confidence, when she wants her life back and decides to do something about it, to get help. Then, unexpectedly, her compulsion to get involved with the addict returns and she goes back to the harmful patterns. Casey describes feeling powerless over everything: drugs, alcohol, people, places and things. Her life seems unmanageable but she is making progress. Her first priority is to stop enabling her partner and to conquer the guilt she feels over this. Casey says she looks forward to the day when "I don't feel guilty about it at all. I have come a long way and I have faith in my own recovery. Today I choose not to enable."

Kerry, another woman with a compulsion to help, tells about her twenty-one-year-old daughter who has been sober for over a year. "She has been going to AA meetings and has had very good attendance. However, only about two months after she started the meetings, an opportunistic man in the group latched on to her and wanted to start dating her. She was pregnant at the time and the baby's father had vanished, leaving her in a very vulnerable position. This new man told my daughter that he wanted to be her baby's 'Godfather' since the biological father was absent. My daughter believed this claim and started dating him. When she asked my opinion about the relationship I told her that I thought she was not ready to start dating, and that a man would prey upon newcomers to AA was not a very honorable person.

"I have almost no family aside from my daughter. She lives in a rental I own. I told her from the start that I would let her stay there for $200.00 a month, but that was only to help her get on her feet, because she was going to be a single parent, with very little income. I told her that if a man moved in, (or anyone else, for that matter) I would have to charge her the rent that I would charge anyone else— $400.00 per month. She said she understood, but soon her new boyfriend moved in. She tried to hide it from me, but eventually I found out he was staying there and told her that her rent was now going to be $400.00 per month. She became very mad at me and accused me of trying to sabotage her relationship. Now she says she broke up with the him, but that she is going to move away because she doesn't want me 'running her life anymore.'"

Kerry lets us see how difficult it has been to stand back from her daughter's situation and allow the young woman to help herself.

"I have figured out over the last couple of years how to 'detach' myself from my daughter's problems, and let her face her own responsibilities in life. I know I have helped her a lot, but I tried to do so only when she was trying to get her life together, and not bail her out of her own mistakes. But since her baby was born, I have done most of the raising of the child. My daughter works nights, and I have been babysitting at night while she is working and during the day while she is sleeping. I am extremely attached to my little grandson and my daughter knows it.

"Tonight, my daughter was here, and we got into an argument over a pacifier, believe it or not. I bought some toys and supplies for the baby and told my daughter that they were to stay at my house.

Otherwise everything seems to end up at her house and I have nothing to care for the baby. My daughter doesn't bring many of the things the baby needs when I take care of him, so I keep some things at my house—though I realize that my daughter should be the one to furnish the things the baby needs. Tonight she started to leave with 'my' pacifier and string attachment and I told her it needed to stay here. She said she wasn't going to leave it here, and started to walk out the door, and I pulled it off the baby's shirt. I didn't hurt my grandson. In fact, he laughed at me when I did it. But my daughter said I had 'abused' him. Anyway, to make a long story short, my daughter says that I will never see my grandson again, and that when she moves she will see to it that I will never have contact with them. I am heart-broken.

"Whenever my daughter gets mad at me for something, she tries to use the baby against me. This has happened many times before. But this time, I really don't know if I will see my grandson again. Do I have a right to feel heart-broken about this, or is it just another sign of my codependency? Sometimes I am not sure if my feelings are warranted, because I have this problem. I have a beautiful grandson and he means the world to me. I know that sometimes people try to relive their lives through their children or grandchildren, but I don't believe this is what I am doing. Perhaps I am not seeing this objectively enough. I just know that since I don't have any family, to speak of, my children and grandchild are very important to me. Obviously, my daughter is trying to use my grandson to control me, to make me act the way she wants. I want to resist her manipulative behavior, and I have no problem in just letting her move out and face life and its responsibilities on her own. I recognize that she has needed to do this for some time now. But I don't want to lose my grandson."

Sean told me that he had reached the point where he knew you cannot convince someone to leave an abusive relationship, even the sister he loved.

"My sister is involved with a very controlling, manipulative man. She is a wonderful, smart, beautiful woman who is too kind for her own good and seems to attract very needy, emotionally abusive men. After wasting away ten years of her life in an emotionally abusive, financially draining relationship, she is now in her third year in another similarly unhealthy relationship, one that seems even worse than the last one. Her latest boyfriend works only sporadically and is chronically unemployed. I'm afraid that she has allowed him to put her into some serious debt. After spending a weekend with her in the beginning of their relationship, I couldn't help but notice that she paid for everything. When I questioned her about it, she denied what she was doing and told me that her boyfriend pays for lots of things.

"When they first became involved, he had no car, so she became his taxi and had to work around his schedule! She took him to and from work (when he worked) and on weekends she picked up his daughter. Her health suffered from the constant service she was providing for him for free, but she would never admit that she was being used, or even complain about his endless demands. When he finally bought himself a car he had her insure it under her name, with her as the driver. I believe he did this because he had his license suspended due to non-payment of child support. She always defends him and takes responsibility for everything, regardless of her own well-being.

"How can I explain how dangerous this is for her to do, when she won't even admit that she's doing it? Her boyfriend plays on her very giving nature and manages to get her sympathy. He demands her constant attention and called her constantly before they moved in together. Sometimes he called in the middle of the night, not even considering that he might disturb someone's sleep. He would demand my sister go to see him, whenever he 'needed' her, even when she was really sick. He told her if she really loved him, she would be there for him because he gets too lonely without her! She seems to like his neediness, sometimes even bragging about it, confusing this manipulation as love for her. He tries to isolate her from everyone who loves her, by openly hating our mother and complaining about all of her friends, finding reasons not to want to hang around any of them. If anyone tries to question her about him or warn her, she gets very defensive.

"If her boyfriend doesn't get her a birthday gift or even a card, she excuses it, saying he doesn't express affection through material things. But she will go further into debt to splurge on him. His own sister even warned my sister right from the start about how manipulative her brother is, but she did not listen to her or to anyone else, including the mother of his child, who had to throw him in jail for lack of child support. All my sister sees is the good in him (whatever that may be).

"It seems that my sister is hoping that she can change this man by loving him, but he can do almost anything and she tolerates it. This is so frustrating for me to see her go through this again. But she never complains to me about any of his faults. In fact, my sister is unaware that I even know what I know, as she wants desperately for me to be in the dark about this guy. I thought that even though codependents have a very hard time leaving, they still try to vent to their friends/family. I have talked to her friends and they all tell me the same thing, that she never complained, in all the thirteen years, to them either! All she says is how great he is! I am afraid if I bring up anything, she will get defensive and it will make matters worse. I am really worried now, because he seems to be getting desperate to keep her. She recently lost a lot of weight in response to his incessant nagging about her figure, and now he keeps telling her of his fear that she will dump him since she lost the weight! He keeps pressing her to marry him right away. In fact, she told me that he wants them to sneak off and elope, but she made me promise not to tell anyone. Is there anything I can do before she makes a huge mistake and marries him?"

Jocelyn, who comes from a dysfunctional family, is beginning to have insight into how she became codependent.

"My father was sexually abusive to me and my two sisters and brother for years. When my mother found out she went into a horrible state of depression, my father went to prison, and a few months later my mother committed suicide. My siblings and I were put into foster care, but when my father got out of jail he somehow regained custody of us. The sexual abuse continued until he finally returned us to the foster-care system. We were in and out of foster homes for several years, until some relatives on my mother's side of the family found out where we were and took us into their homes.

"Since my first marriage at age eighteen, I have been married four times; all husbands have had some sort of addiction and have had controlling personalities. I'm not sure, but I'm beginning to think I'm codependent. A number of people in my family are addicts. I have been to some ALANON meetings, but they make me uncomfortable and I cry a lot.

"I raised my son by myself mostly, and without child support, and I thought I had done a good job. But now he is in jail for drunk driving and I have learned he is an alcoholic and has been using designer drugs. This is the third time he has been in jail in less than a year. So far he shows no signs of changing his behavior. I want to help him, but I don't want to enable him. My son is twenty-four years old, with no job, no money, and now, no car. I know he doesn't want to be this way. He says he can't control his urge to drink. What can I do to help him without hurting myself?"

Cheryl is someone who grew up with alcoholics all around her and is married to one. She recently realized that she has been a long-time enabler of her husband without even realizing what she was doing. She assumed sole responsibility for communication and emotional issues in their relationship, until, exhausted by this burden, she "gave up." Cheryl says, "I stopped following him around and making him talk to me. I stopped looking after him emotionally and otherwise."

Without her constant care and support, Cheryl's husband turned to someone else for the attention he craved, a woman he had known in the past. At first he claimed that he was just looking for someone to talk to, but it soon became much more. He never planned to tell his wife; she found out accidentally. When Cheryl confronted him, he unleashed a list of complaints about his job, their marriage and his life in general. After meeting with a counselor, he changed his tactics, claiming that he didn't want to lose her and that it was important to him to work on improving their marriage. According to Cheryl, "he says the problem is that the 'specialness' in our relationship hadn't been there for a long time. The fact that he never worked to keep that 'specialness' didn't occur to him. I don't know if I can get past the fact that rather than working on our marriage or coming to me with the fact that he was so unhappy, he turned to someone else. At one time, we did have something very special but it definitely takes two people to keep a marriage going and I do not want to go back to being the only one in it."

Cheryl says that the problems in her marriage are compounded by her husband's dysfunctional family, the members of which have tried to drive them apart. Cheryl is proud of herself for standing up to these relatives and refusing to play games or enable anyone, but this has created serious problems in her relationship with her husband, problems that she is not sure they can fix.

Even though the person who is a codependent needs to take the steps toward independence, finding a group of people that he or she can talk to is important. Samuel says he has been driving himself crazy trying to deal with his issues on his own.

"I'm thirty-seven years old, a single dad, divorced for a year. I spent ten years in a verbally/emotionally abusive marriage. It was a bitter pill to swallow when I realized that I was her enabler. I enabled her, because I tolerated her abuse, and excused it as part of her 'healing process.' (She was sexually abused by her stepfather for several years.) I passed off all of her controlling actions as a part of her getting better, and for the longest time I didn't realize that nothing was changing. She attended counseling for a little while, which helped a bit. However, that only lasted for a year or so before she went back to her old ways.

"From the beginning, there were things I should have seen, and understood as signs that our relationship would be troubled. But I was blind in my need to be needed... in my belief that I could fix this person, that I could help her, that I could make her better. That is what she was looking for. And in me, she found it all. Someone willing to sacrifice everything he had, his career, his potential, everything for her. And I did so, because she needed me. I'll never forget the day I realized that it wasn't me that she needed, it was just someone who would make excuses for her, someone who would kowtow to her whims and desires.

"From the beginning, I should have seen what was coming. Anything that I liked, that gave me pleasure, was worthless. My friends were people I shouldn't hang out with. I was in trouble if I so much as spoke to another woman, even at work. I couldn't see my friends after work, couldn't go by the club to visit. I had to be home to watch her children so she could go out. Let me be five minutes late and I was damned, but she was not to be held accountable to me for her time. I had considered leaving before, but couldn't bring myself to do it. I was always hoping that there was a breakthrough right around the corner, even though nothing changed. I hoped that one day she'd wake up and realize how much she was hurting me, although looking back, I think she knew and relished the power it gave her.

"Gradually, I began to see the situation for what it really was. Her comments became more cutting, and, I believe, more true to her real feelings. Finally she told me that the only reason she stayed with me was because she needed me to take care of the children. Suddenly I realized that that was exactly what I was doing, all by myself. There was no joint effort; I was doing practically everything, and I wasn't happy about it.

"Soon after that she stopped saying 'I love you.' I kept saying it for a while, until I realized that no matter how many times I said it, she'd never return it. She began to get angry at me for no reason at all. She would stomp out of the house and get in her car and disappear for longer and longer periods at a time. I suggested she might need to get therapy, but got the cold shoulder for that. She also refused to go to a marriage counselor with me.

"The climax came just before my last birthday. She had recently lost her job, and hadn't sought unemployment, hadn't done anything. Her sister came to visit and they went out every night. When I went to balance the checkbook, I found checks missing, and discovered that she had been running two checkbooks and hiding her purchases. Together, she and her sister had spent over a thousand dollars in a week. For the first time, I got mad, and she knew it. She hit me with every emotional ploy she could think of. I told her that I was sick and tired of hearing those empty, idle threats and that if

anything was going to change, she was going to have to do something. She responded with 'If you don't like the way we're living, you
can leave.' And suddenly I realized that she didn't care if I left or not.
She had no emotional investment in our relationship. I moved out a
month and a half later, the divorce went through a year after that.
Now I'm working part-time and going to school full-time."

But Samuel feels terribly alone. He needs, as perhaps you do
too, to join a group therapy situation to help with these feelings.

Annette, who is just coming out of an eight-year relationship,
has similar needs. She was involved with a man who has a drinking
and drug problem. She spent several years just trying to ignore the
violence and negative attitude caused by his addictions. She asked
him not to come see her when he was drunk or high, but whenever
he did, she was too intimidated to confront him about it. She
remembers spending every day hoping that he would see he had a
problem and get help. Annette relates the incident that finally
opened her eyes:

"I had just gotten home from my second job and was tired. He
started his ranting and the next thing I knew we were arguing and
he busted the screen out of my new storm door. Then he tossed me
into the counter in my kitchen. That was when I told him to get out
of my life."

Despite standing up for herself against her partner's physical
aggression, Annette still has problems with codependency. She is
having second thoughts because she is afraid to be alone. She knows
she should avoid this man, but fears that she will end up going back
to him eventually. She admits that she feels sorry for him because he
has a disease and she knows he needs help. Though Annette has
moved from a poisonous situation, she still feels guilty and is in need
of support.

Cara's neediness stems from childhood.

"I don't at all blame my mother for living her life the way she
does, I just don't like the way she has no sense of consequence. I have
been feeling this way since I was very young. I am angry that she has
no family values and gave me little direction while I was growing up.

I am angry that she is not supportive of my sister and me as adults. I am angry that she doesn't stand up to her husband and insist he learn to control his temper well enough to stay in one place long enough to build a family situation and be part of a community. I am angry that she just let us go out into the world without making sure we have a stable home to come back to. The part that angers me the most is that she has no idea that she is doing all this, because she has no goals or aspirations beyond survival. Financially or emotionally she has never been stable. I don't think she even knows why she chose to have children, and that is the most unfortunate effect her life has had on me.

"The only thing I know to do for my mother is to write her emails periodically, because she is not honest with me at all when we talk on the phone. She always seems happy, but inside I know that she is not. I don't know how she survives the day. She must be so lonely. My father is not a good companion for her. He scares me, a lot, but my mother doesn't even care! I don't appreciate the way he treats me at all and I hardly feel safe from him although I live many miles away in a foreign country.

"My mother is not able to understand my ambition because she dropped out of college after her first year. Once she told me, during one of the most emotionally unstable and unsure weekends of my life, to drop out of the university I had been attending for three years and come home, that she would love me and take care of me. I wanted to believe this, but not six months later she sold the house, dumped all my belongings in a dormitory at my new school, and left with her husband.

"The way I feel about my mother is really sad because I would like to have and love a mother who is stable, who listens, understands, helps and knows me. Someone who is strong and upright and has integrity. Someone who I DON'T have to mother myself and who doesn't criticize. Someone who gives me hope that there is a good world. Someone who is informed and cares about the consequences of her actions. Someone who has visible goals and aspirations. Someone I feel proud to bring my own family to visit."

Although Cara is still struggling with her codependency sickness, she has become more active in her church and found sustenance in religion.

Alicia has gained insight through reading and studying and now believes what she thought of as her close relationship with her husband could best be described as being enmeshed. Once, she thought they were best friends.

"It is in this light that I struggled to accept him and the situation when he began to see other women. He was my best friend and he needed this and I would understand. (It was of course spiced with a large slice of self-doubt, self-blame, self-hate.) He has had this relationship for six years. He had a dream that we would all be one family, the three of us. I tried to go along, get along, and make the best of it. She had been an acquaintance before and I thought that perhaps, since my husband needed this so much, I could live with it. Coming from an alcoholic home, I am well accustomed to putting things in the best light, making do. Well, I can't make do any more. I am ashamed. I am angry and I am fed up. Their relationship is the biggest non-secret secret in our circle of friends and relations. I want a partner, not a child-adult that can't bear to be alone and cannot be considerate or sensitive. He says I am obsessed with this one aspect of our relationship and I should look at all the other good things that we have. For me the other good things are being tainted and overrun by this situation. It is not like someone likes baseball and you don't so when he goes to games with the guys, you go to a movie alone. This is boundaries and security and safety and self-esteem being bulldozed by an inappropriate relationship that threatens our marriage."

All of the people in this chapter have struggled and are struggling with many elements of codependency: making excuses, enabling, self-blame and recriminations. The important element they have avoided is facing the reality of their past family ties and their intimate partnerships.

For me, and perhaps you, being able to both fully see and face the truth is a critical juncture in recognizing, healing or ending codependence.

◀ 5 ▶

Fairy Tales and Our Youth: Delusions of Grandeur

The other day I dragged my young son to see *A Cinderella Story* with America's next teeny bop role model, the skinny, beautiful, blonde and talented, perfect in every way, Hilary Duff. To be quite fair, I'd just subjected myself to the current He Man movie *I, Robot* for my son, so it *was* my turn to pick. I'm a sucker for love and happily ever after. As my son and I sat in our (my) favorite seats—the ones in the front row with the bar to rest my feet on—I glanced about to see an audience teeming with teen girls, giddy and gossipy, giggling about fluff just like I did when I was oh-so-young and innocent. My son was certain they were laughing at him, but I pointed out that there were at least three other males in the audience of hundreds, grudgingly holding their girlfriends' hands, gruesome pain apparent on their faces. I wasn't the only cruel woman in the place, I assure you.

As the lights went down I speculated as to whether this generation of girls would bring about strong role models, women of substance, unafraid to speak out and to survive on their own terms. Contemplating the many futures scattered about me, I turned to look at my own son, whispering into my cell phone to my boyfriend about the agony of being in a room with two hundred chattering girls. How will my boys turn out? Will they be doormats? Will they be control freaks? Neither, I hope. While I work on myself, I have started working on a pre-emptive strike plan for my sons so they will grow up to be non-codependent. But that day my attention kept returning to the girls. I wished I could speak to their moms and tell them to teach their daughters to be strong and assertive, teach them what I wasn't taught. Tell them every day that they are princesses with or without a prince. They have to know. Instead I prayed for their strength, and yours.

The movie, whose plot was about a modern day Cinderella, was deliciously, sinfully pleasurable, complete with the poor girl treated badly by her dysfunctional family, falling in love with the requisite hunk, only to be thwarted by jealous girls who insist they are better than the lowly one. I caught my breath every time the prince lowered his sexy eyes and spoke in his husky voice. Of course, in the end, love survived and I bawled along with the rest of the girls in the audience. My son shook his head, embarrassed by his mother. And while the makers of this new version of the classic intended to make a stronger, more independent Cinderella (she goes on to Princeton in addition to becoming her prince's love slave), the basics of the story are the same: Without her man, she was unfinished. She became whole when he realized he loved her too. And whether or not the rest of the audience realized the underlying subtext, the subtle undertones of this fairy tale and countless others pervade young girls' lives, shaping them from needy young girls into needy young women.

Our great grandmothers read the old version of similar stories when they were little girls. According to Terry Windling, a scholar on the subject of fairy tale literature,

> The old fairy tales had much to say on the subjects of heroism and transformation; about how one finds the courage to fight and prevail against overwhelming odds. They are tales of children abandoned in the woods; of daughters handed poisoned apples; of sons forced to betray their siblings; of men and women struck down by wolves or imprisoned in windowless towers. In early times such tales were passed down through the generations by word of

mouth, woman to woman, mother to child—using arche-
types as a mirror held to daily life… particularly the lives of
those without clear avenues of social power. [1]

Various names, assorted plotlines, but all with the same basic
premise and character makeup. Needy girl, evil woman, handsome
prince and an inept, unavailable king who stays in the background,
probably too busy working, drinking and carousing. Over generations, women have been taught by such tales to wait for glorious
male heroes, those who will "fight and prevail against overwhelming odds," rather than to rely on themselves and look for their own
solutions. Rapunzel, with glorious golden hair, put into a castle by
an ugly jealous woman, saved by a royal suitor. Only he could ascertain that her hair could be woven into a ladder, which only he could
climb to rescue her forever. She just wasn't quite smart enough, I
suppose, or inclined to put forth any effort.

From the time we are able to understand language, females are
told tales that give us our first look into gender identity and the
dynamics of male-female relationships and how we are to act and
react based on those biological specifications. We are taught, subconsciously at the least, how to fit in with others and how the
schemata of relationships work. Men are also taught by these stories. They must be providers, women the nurturers and girls the
helpless trophies on pedestals.[1] Should you be unfortunate enough
to be unsightly and a woman, you are relegated to being the ugly
stepsister or villainous stepmother roles. Brains in no way factor into
these stories. In many fairy tales, women have to sacrifice their iden-
tities and desires to have men, who invariably must save them. The
plot is the same in every story: Needy girl is beautiful. Evil woman
is jealous of girl and thwarts her with a malicious deed that only the
handsome prince can undo. The father is usually out of the picture,
working three jobs and two mistresses.

Young girls, when reading these stories, learn that their value
lies in their appearance and that appearances can be a clear indicator of character and behavior. In other words, someone who looks
good… is good. Snow White and Sleeping Beauty, after having been

found to be the most beautiful women in their respective kingdoms, are both hexed by jealous older women and can only be saved by knights in shining armor. Each woman is bound to love and live happily ever after with the first man who gives her that promised kiss, no questions asked, just grateful to be rescued by a prince. Reading about how Cinderella waits for a chivalrous prince to seek her out based on the loveliness of her tiny foot, young girls are conditioned to follow the same model. Women fight each other for men's affections, putting themselves through pain and agony to become what they think men are looking for. Fitting a size nine foot into a size six shoe sounds ridiculous, but women do worse every day. Diets of the day are followed, and not for friends' approval. For men's approval. Because I liked getting "the eye" from guys when I was looking attractive, it took a guy's second glance to make me feel good about myself. Despite my training and experience and even though my significant other says he loves me "as is," I still have tinges of unworthy feelings when skinnier girls are around. I spend eighty dollars quarterly keeping my hair blond and two hundred dollars a year on contacts (because princesses don't wear glasses) and jog when I really want to sit and relax. Like many other females, I want to please a society raised on Cinderella.

And while I point out the prejudices put upon young women, I feel how difficult it must be for young males to step into the role of sword-wielding, dragon-slaying knights. Men who are taught to be controllers often find the strain enormous, as we've seen in several of the stories related. Young boys become caught up in the idea that they must be chivalrous, the savior to females, and that girls are defenseless and needy. Drinking and fighting are part of this persona. Caught up in their own parts in these stories, they are also fooled into thinking that traits such as beauty, meekness and submissiveness are the characteristics that make women attractive and desirable as wives or partners. Through these stories, boys are taught to treat women almost as another species, not strong and active like themselves, but weak and having to endure and compete for the fickle attentions of men.[2]

Among the female traits emphasized and perpetuated by fairy tales are domesticity, meekness, sensitivity, gossiping, nurturing, silence and submissiveness. They fill the role of damsel in distress. Masculine traits include bravery, daring, power, logic, pride and vigor. In other words, males are taught to want to be the personification of that old image of knights in shining armor.

Keeping these traits in mind we can see why our world isn't teeming with independent women and chivalrous men. Just being subjected to the ideas of limited roles of men and women is not enough to propel someone into codependency, but is certainly part of the equation. When substance abuse, physical, verbal and mental abuse and codependent family members are added to the equation, the results are staggering. Being raised with strong family values in homes where women are equal partners and children are praised and encouraged to excel generally nullifies to some degree the stereotyping found in fairy tales. Unfortunately, the family figures in dysfunctional homes do not embody empowering characteristics and young children who live within these homes do not have effective role models.

Part

◀ 2 ▶

Strengthening
Our Weaknesses

◀ 6 ▶

Stories of How We Stay
When We Should Leave

The partner who is in the subservient role often neither wants to nor can relinquish his or her need for a relationship. This may go on and despite very abusive conditions, continuing until either the submissive partner seeks help or, for one reason or another, the controlling partner leaves.

Lily was a codependent who finally got the help she needed. She describes her experiences growing up with an alcoholic mother by saying it was like living with "Jekyll and Hyde." Lily's mother spent years telling her daughter how she did things wrong and was a disappointment. According to Lily, "I did years of therapy on it."

Lily thought her life was normal, though. She got into drugs and alcohol as a teenager and by age twenty-three, realized she had a lot of problems. Part of Lily's family was involved in AA and Alanon and suggested she go there for help. She started at Alanon but quickly discovered her own alcoholic addiction and got sober. But she still thought that her family and childhood were normal and that her father's alcoholism didn't affect her that much, as she didn't live with him. Eventually Lily became unable to deal with her suppressed emotions and entered therapy.

Lily says of her younger self, "Though I originally thought my life was pretty good... I had low self-esteem. I made poor choices. I never stood up for myself and put everyone before me. I was so needy for love, attention, affection and I would pick men who ignored me. I did whatever they wanted to get what I needed."

As she progressed in therapy, Lily began to learn why she felt this way. And she began to connect with the emotions that were "below" all the explanations she gave for her own behavior, such as blaming things that happened on other people or bad luck.

Lily found out that she had some core beliefs about herself that stemmed from not getting certain things she needed as a child. However, she also learned that she needed to grieve those losses, forgive her parents, move on and realize that she is now responsible for herself and for improving her own life.

Lily goes on to tell us how her low self-esteem and early training contributed to her problem.

"I was not aware of these deep-seated 'core' beliefs because I could not be, or I could not survive. Beliefs: I am unlovable. I am not important. Everyone is more important than me. I am worthless. I am not good enough. I do not matter. No one is there for me or ever will be. How did I get this? It wasn't really my father, though I know now I have plenty of stuff from him. It was my mom. She put everything before me. She favored my sister. She sent me off to boarding school because I didn't get along with my stepfather. I was alone most of the time growing up. I made my own breakfast, and often my own dinner (mainly frozen meals). I watched TV alone. I had no one to tell about how I was being teased in school (I didn't think they would care, or worse, would agree with the kids in school). Mom was off playing tennis or traveling a lot with my step dad. He was a builder and the houses we lived in put our rooms far from theirs even. I didn't have a curfew or many rules.

"Mom taught me some things... like that men did matter. Everything was about getting a man. She actually said things like 'if you're fat, no one will love you' (a therapist once asked me if this was something she implied or actually said. Said). Everything was also about how things 'looked'—the perfect clothes, house, car, job, kids, haircut and so on."

In therapy Lily learned how much she was affected by her experiences growing up and began to learn, and more importantly, believe, that she is a worthwhile person who can care for herself and stand up for herself.

We can put ourselves first. It is all right to ask for what you need from healthier, loving people who have the capacity to give it or to say no when they need to. You don't have to listen to anyone and accept treatment that gives the message that you are worthless. It is enough to know this for yourself, as Lily now does. And it is not necessary to convince anyone else who does not know it.

Lily feels that she has learned to care for herself, instead of giving everyone else power over her and how she feels about herself.

"I know full well now when my core issues are coming into play. Sometimes it's a 'straight shot' where I get triggered and can feel that source of pain with no clutter. It's great to be aware, but it can hurt."

Lily goes on to describe her recovery process.

"I have been working a lot and not doing all those little things to take care of myself. It is my conscious choice to continue a relationship with my alcoholic mother; however, it requires that I keep myself in good spiritual and emotional condition to handle her tantrums and not let them hurt me.

"Monday night we were talking and she started to slip in some critical comments. I let them slide. But then she wanted me to do something, and I didn't have time to do it on her schedule. I told her that I could be available to help her on the following day but she started a tirade of how I'm never there for her, etc. This time, I countered and pointed out that her request was last minute and I had a previous commitment. I was sorry if that disappointed her but the best I could do would be to come over the next day. Yet after more of her pressuring comments, I agreed to alter my schedule for her.

"Then we began arguing about something else, and I continued to confront her with her illogical and immature comments. She started screaming 'I hate you, I hate you' and hung up. I shook it off, but later, something happened with my boyfriend... a minor incident in which I was trying to get something I wanted without directly asking and didn't get it.

"When I was lying in bed trying to fall asleep it hit me... this horrible feeling. I realized that I had gone back to my old habits. I had agreed to my mother's schedule, and I had been manipulative with my boyfriend rather than directly asking for something. I felt nauseous. I got up and paced then connected with the core beliefs and pain. It was horrible and wonderful at the same time.... to have the awareness, so quickly now, that I am not taking care of myself. And what it can do to me inside if I don't."

Lily admits that she still feels sad sometimes about her childhood and the effects it has had on her life as an adult. She feels, as you might, that she has a deficit for which she will always have to compensate. Yet at the same time, she is grateful that she has been able to discover her damaging behaviors and beliefs so that she could begin to change. Once you admit to yourself that you have a problem and that you want to change, then it is possible to make positive choices in the future.

Sylvia grew up in a seriously dysfunctional family. Her father was an alcoholic who would come home from his drinking binges and start fights with her mother, sometimes ending in physical violence. Sylvia remembers being very scared when her father came home because she could never know what sort of mood he would be in. She recalls sitting with her mother in her room, begging her not to talk to her father when he was drunk. Eventually Sylvia's father began to beat her mother. She remembers running to neighbor's house in her pajamas one night, trying to get help for her mother. When these types of incidents occurred, the police would come and force Sylvia's father to leave, but a few days later her mother would let him back in and the whole cycle was repeated, getting a little bit worse each time.

Sylvia is aware that she did not have a normal childhood. From an early age she felt that she had to take care of her mother after her parents' fights and clean up the messes that they made. There was no time for playing like a typical young child. Sylvia grew up with few friends her own age because her father was in charge of baby-sitting her and took her to bars so he could drink while he "watched" her.

In addition to her father's violence and problems with alcohol, her mother went through serious bouts of depression and anxiety, ending in an addiction to a prescription medication. Sylvia blames much of this problem on her father's belittling and cruel treatment of her mother over the course of years.

Sylvia was extremely relieved when her parents separated permanently, but after the divorce her mother became verbally abusive, telling her daughter that she was "no good" and making derogatory comments about her physical appearance. Sylvia recognizes that her mother was doing the same things that had been done to her by Sylvia's father. Perhaps the most hurtful thing for Sylvia was the way in which her mother began to shut her out emotionally, ignoring her when she tried to talk and refusing to speak to her in return. Sylvia was hurt and frustrated that her mother could shut her out like that, and her anger and resentment towards her mother slowly built until she resorted to physical outbursts to get her mother's attention.

Sylvia tells us of her mother's actions during her teenage years: "She started getting really controlling of me. I couldn't do things with my friends after work or school; I had to come right home. If I didn't, she would lock me out of the house. Sometimes it would be a few days before she'd let me back in. I always felt either locked out or locked up. Being in a house with my own mother not saying a word was driving me crazy. So I turned to drugs to numb the pain I was feeling. When I turned twenty-one she was still telling me I couldn't go out after work. I had to come right home. I understand living with someone else's rules, but I felt that what she was doing was unfair to me. She was holding me back from having my own life. Eventually I was able to save some money and move out to a place of my own. I could not take one more day of living in my mother's house."

Sylvia's mother passed away about seven years ago. She never got a chance to confront her mother about how angry she was with her and how she had been hurt by her mother's actions. After her mother's death Sylvia began experiencing panic attacks and has suffered from social anxiety disorder for several years now. She is currently unable to hold a job or comfortably interact with people and she feels that it is largely due to the experiences she had in childhood.

Shawna has recently realized that her depression and anxiety are the results of neglect, manipulation, verbal and emotional abuse, physical abuse and multiple rapes as a young adult. She describes herself as "new to the recovery process" and has just started therapy.

"Truly, my mother's voice still rings in my ears sometimes, telling me that if I reach out or ask for help, I am just being a 'drama queen.' I feel like I am the only one in my family who sees these things. My sister is aware of some of it, but we are still not allowed to talk about our problems. I have finally been given 'permission' from my therapist not to talk to my parents for a while, until I feel I am ready. I pray that one day I will be able to love them for who they are without needing them to love me back."

Shawna goes on to explain how her religion and faith are helping her to regain a sense of self-worth and to work through her recovery process, but she is still struggling to come to terms with her memories and experiences.

"I tried to separate myself and tell someone what was happening when I was seventeen. I was called a liar, shut up and the secret was put back in the box. Now I am trying to tell again, although I still feel like there are some people whom I cannot tell. I don't want to hurt anyone or destroy what others have. It is scary to be alone in the world. I don't want to tell anyone who knows my parents, because I don't feel that it would accomplish anything except hurting and dishonoring my parents. But I have told my friends openly.

"I don't want to fight about our family situation with my siblings. I don't want to endure being called a liar or see them think that my mother is right, that I'm crazy and dramatic. I don't think it is worth it.

"I have had confrontation fantasies... but the last confrontation I had with my mother when I was seventeen was so unsuccessful— it only beat me down. In some ways I think that I to do this to draw my own boundaries, but I don't think that my family would necessarily respect that. Maybe I've already tried to do this by separating myself from my family as much as possible, so that I can break the patterns of control and codependency."

Donna's childhood also set the stage for her later codependence. The child of two alcoholics, Donna was adopted when she was six months old, and her parents were always very straightforward with her about this. Both of her parents are highly educated, well known and well respected in their fields and the community.

Underneath the respectable façade, however, Donna's childhood was far from idyllic. Her parents both drank heavily, beginning early in the evenings when they got home from work and continuing into the night. They would have frequent arguments, which sometimes erupted into violence. Donna describes for us this upsetting period in her life:

"I recall when I was about eight or nine asking my mother why my parents argued so much. She told me that all husband and wives quarreled and reassured me that their arguments were nothing extraordinary. I decided that if that were the case, I would have nothing to do with marriage when I grew up: I could imagine few more undesirable relationships between two people. (Incidentally, I changed my mind about marriage when I experienced something of a religious conversion in my late teens. I've been married to a wonderful man for almost fourteen years, and we seldom argue.)

"I'm now entering middle age and, like my parents, I'm well educated: I have an M.S. in engineering, an M.A. and Ph.D. in one of the humanities. My humanities training is in the same field as my parents'. I was a precocious child in my field, a characteristic that amazed my mother and, as I now know, threatened my father."

Within the past year or so, Donna began therapy for depression and anxiety. In reflecting on her upbringing, she realized that she knew very little about what had shaped her mother's personality: to what extent might her mother's upbringing have been dysfunctional? Donna decided to explore her mother's past by calling an aunt whom she knew would be candid. As a result, she learned quite a bit—

enough to realize that her mother, too, had come from a dysfunctional family situation. But the bombshell that came out of the conversation with her aunt concerned Donna's father: her aunt recalled a visit to their house when Donna was about seven. During this visit, her father became very angry with her because of some chore she had been asked to do and was not doing well. His response was to belittle Donna, humiliating her with unfavorable comparisons to a cousin who was also visiting. Until her aunt pointed out how awful this treatment was, Donna had always assumed that she deserved the way her father had treated her.

Spurred by this discovery, Donna called another professor, Steve, who had worked under her father in the same department at a university. She was attempting to discern patterns in her father's behavior that would help her to understand what really happened while she was growing up. From this conversation, two things became clear. First, Donna discovered that in some exceptional situations, her father was not above belittling and humiliating the people who were under him. This revealed a pattern of behavior in him that Donna had also seen in his dealings with her. Second, she learned of ways that he had actively worked—unbeknownst to his daughter—to thwart her progress in his field of the humanities while she was growing up. As it happened, when Donna was about seventeen years old, Steve had tutored her for a short time in his sub field. At first she made slow progress. Then, suddenly, she began to take off and was doing some rather astonishing work for a seventeen-year-old. At this point, the tutoring sessions with Steve suddenly broke off. Donna never received a satisfactory explanation from her father. Did Steve doubt her talent and recommend that she stop? Or was there some conflict between Steve and her father? Now, more than twenty years later, Donna was able to ask Steve what had happened. He told her that her father suspended the tutoring sessions because she had lost interest! She knew immediately that her father had lied to Steve: not only had she not lost interest, but she was profoundly disappointed that the tutoring sessions had stopped.

After these conversations, Donna began to realize many things about her father. A therapist had once suggested that her father reacted as he had because he feared competition from his daughter.

Donna originally dismissed that suggestion, because she really couldn't see how that could have been the case. But now it all begin to make sense to her, as she discovered a pattern in which her teachers would recognize how gifted she was and her father, in turn, would tell her that she wasn't. When Donna was considering college, her teachers encouraged her to apply to the top schools in the field; her father, of course, would have nothing of it. He sat down with her during her senior year and spelled out a very unsatisfactory destiny for his daughter: she would attend the small university where her father taught, and upon graduation she would become a high school teacher. He also told her that no matter how hard she worked, Donna didn't have the talent to make it in his field.

Donna followed her father's discouraging advice:

"I went along with this and ended up majoring in the sciences—to which my parents had been pushing me, despite my lack of interest. I had little motivation to do well in the sciences, but I was smart enough (and the school was easy enough) to get by with a B average. At the end of my junior year in college, I began working harder in my studies and managed to make high marks during my senior year.

"I began applying to graduate schools in engineering. I got into all the schools to which I applied and received assistantships from them. The top school to which I had applied was way across the country, while another school—not as good—was within six hours of my parents. My dad pressured me to go to the closer one, and I gave in—I believe he wanted me relatively close so that he would be able to control me.

"When I got to graduate school in engineering, I crashed academically. I was just miserable there, because I really wanted to be in the humanities. Nevertheless, I barely managed to finish my master's degree in two years. At that point, I continued to live in the college town where I had undertaken my graduate studies as I began a job search. My father called me on the phone and angrily insisted that I come back home and attempt to get a job in a metropolitan area about much closer to him, where there was a high concentration of technical opportunities. I resisted—not least because I didn't want to go there. Eventually, I landed a job that moved me farther from my parents."

After working four years as an engineer, Donna was stressed out and miserable. She had gotten engaged, but soon realized that the relationship was not going to work. She was confused and depressed. She knew that the problem was career-related and immediately made plans to return to graduate school in the humanities.

Given her lack of experience in the field she had chosen, Donna was unable to get into a top graduate program in the field. Instead she ended up getting into a third-tier institution with a nice fellowship. She was able to impress the faculty tremendously, but turned out to be very unhappy there. She began to plan to leave and go somewhere else. A number of professors encouraged her to apply to Harvard. When she told her father about these plans, however, he angrily told her not to go, to stay where she was and finish her degree. Primarily because of her father's lack of support, Donna dropped her plans to leave. Instead she continued to stay, unhappily, where she was for six more years. Only after leaving (with her dissertation unfinished) and moving to a more congenial location did she really get motivated to finish her dissertation.

Donna is currently having great difficulty finding employment in her field, a fact which she partially attributes to her father's restrictive guidance and limiting advice. She is now working in a different field which is more lucrative than an academic position would be, but feels unhappy and alienated. She is often anxious and depressed. As she struggles to build her confidence and improve her career, she says that she can only hope that she will not spend the rest of her life paying for her father's insecurities.

Alison is also dealing with some of the feelings of self-doubt common to codependents. Much of her negative self-image is due to teasing and bullying that she endured due to her physical appearance.

"Right up until about junior high school, I was not only the fattest kid in the class, I was also the tallest. While there was one little girl (who is now an anorexic) who insisted on calling me 'hippo hips' and tried to get everyone in the accelerated class to hate me (with very little success), by and large I never endured much teasing as a kid. The teasing came later, in high school when I wasn't so active (for fear of getting undressed for gym and for fear of being labeled a tomboy because I liked sports).

"I had lots of friends in high school, but I never went on a single date. I didn't have my first boyfriend until my sophomore year of college, and even that didn't last for very long. As I became more interested in school, I had less time to exercise and the pounds started sneaking up on me. It wasn't really until I was in my twenties that I started getting rude comments from strangers, and when I did I was perplexed, because I didn't really see myself as fat, though at a size twenty-four (at the time) I certainly was. These days I get the various 'fatso' comments hurled at me from passing cars at least once a week and I have to say I'm not strong enough to give back a witty retort. I just internalize it, which makes me feel worse and makes me dislike myself even more. It's amazing how continued exposure to something negative can change a person who had a pretty decent opinion of herself."

Martin is a male who is fighting low self-esteem.

"You know what the worst feeling is? Worse than losing your job one week before your girlfriend dumps you? It's that feeling that you'll never find anyone else again. I tell you, I must be invisible when it comes to the opposite sex. The few women I do interact with wind up being my friend. They feel I'm more of a big brother to them than anything. I know I can treat a girl right, but my stupid self-esteem screams at me that I'm not their type because I don't make enough money, or that because I still live at home they will think I'm immature. This is a really big problem for me."

Growing up, Martin felt that his mother was very overprotective, always trying to prevent him from getting hurt. In addition, his grandmother, who helped raise him, had some very controlling behaviors. As a child, Martin wasn't allowed to interact with other children his own age. He had only his brother and another child that his grandmother baby-sat, but his grandmother did not allow him to play with this child, as he was "no good." At school, Martin didn't know how to interact with his peers, so when his feelings were hurt or others laughed at him, he didn't know how to stand up for himself. He still has trouble with this as an adult.

As he got older, Martin's situation started to improve somewhat. His stepfather persuaded his mother to allow him to play soccer, but he continued to feel a lack of parental support. His stepfather spent a lot of time on the computer, and his mother claimed to be too tired or too busy to take him to soccer practice and other activities.

Martin tells us how his family environment affected his ability to fit in at school and his resulting problems:

"The years passed and the lack of parental support continued, and all of a sudden I was walking into the dreaded dungeon of junior high. I was not a skinny kid. In fact, because my grandma got me to believe that you had to eat EVERYTHING on your plate, I have never been a normal weight, except those few years as a toddler. At my new school, the merging place of several elementary schools, the guys seemed to be getting bigger, and the girls a whole lot prettier, but I was this kid going through puberty, developing at a normal rate, but still fat. You know I've been plagued with those dreaded (yes, you can laugh at this) man boobs. Those horrible deposits of fat that just won't go away unless you lose at least fifty pounds. Throughout junior high, my appearance depressed me. It still bothers me today. One teacher caught on to my depression, but because I was so embarrassed, I always lied and said things like, 'No I'm okay, just concentrating on things,' or, 'I just don't feel well. I think I'm coming down with another cold.' I never trusted anyone with my depression."

Martin's mother and stepfather ignored his depression and negative self-image and did nothing to halt the teasing and ridicule that he endured at school. He both wanted and needed more encouragement from his family, but never received it. Instead he was criticized and punished for his perceived shortcomings and received no praise for his achievements.

Martin continues to explain how the disapproval he faced at home was echoed by his peers and even teachers.

"For three years of junior high, I was always picked on. I never interacted with any of the girls, because I felt gross or too embarrassed by what the other guys would say to me. Gym class was terrible. I would wait until everyone was out of the locker room to change. If I changed when the other guys were in there, they would always tease me about my fat, or grab my man boobs. The touching and the teasing really got to me. Several different times throughout junior high, I would get embarrassed by most of the kids in front of the whole class. Even my science teacher put me on the spot, by asking me if I was on medication because I was the only quiet one in class when the rest were rowdy and misbehaving. Having a teacher ask me that not only scared me, but also embarrassed me because the class laughed at me. I dropped the class the next day. I got punished when my parents found out I had three weeks of truancies, but I didn't want to be embarrassed like that ever again, and no one would listen to my problems."

Martin's self-esteem was never built up to make him feel good about himself and worthy of respectful treatment.

Jared, another male codependent, had similar experiences growing up: "It's a little hard to explain what I expected out of my parents as a kid, but if I were to snap my fingers and have it changed, I would have my mother and father together, I'd have a dad who would encourage me to have my friends over and we'd do lots of fun things together. Things like going to a baseball game, camping, fishing or to the beach. I think that's how I lost most of my friends. My mom always complained about them being over. She always drilled them and asked them, 'Do your mom and dad make you keep your room clean too?' I think the best thing that anyone could have done for me back then would have been to encourage me to socialize and to have fun with other kids.

"My friends didn't care about my weight. And maybe if they thought that I was a good guy with a good family, I wouldn't be so invisible. Maybe those friends from back then would feel more comfortable with me being around them. I think I can sum up most of my problems, however, in my lack of a father figure. I still don't know much about sports or typical 'guy stuff.' Sometimes I don't even feel like I'm a guy. I don't feel like a woman either, but I don't know 'guy' things. Sometimes I don't feel like I belong because of that, and that's probably why I don't have many male friends my age, although I do get along with guys who are slightly older."

Angie also feels that her problems with codependency stem from an abusive childhood and as an adult has found herself staying in difficult or damaging relationships as a result. Her father was an alcoholic who beat her and her mother. In an attempt to get attention from adults, Angie acted out at school and became the victim of an intolerant and abusive teacher as well.

As a young woman, Angie pulled away from her parents and made an effort to start anew. Unfortunately, as a codependent, she soon became involved in a draining relationship of a different kind.

"I went to work in Los Angeles and met an older man, a drug addict, alcoholic burned-out hippie on the bus on the way there. I foolishly fell for him and he talked me into quitting my job and going to live with him in Texas. I'm convinced that he never did love me. He used me for my money, made me write checks for him, made me go to doctors and emergency rooms and play sick to get various pain relievers for his addiction, screamed at me and dominated me. Four months later he said I would have to go back to Indiana and he would work, make some money and send for me.

"I was so naïve. I still loved him and I stood by him and fell for his lies. He put me on the bus and called me at my parents', pretending to miss me, but all he wanted was more money. He called just enough times to get some out of me, and then disappeared. His family lied for him when I called. When I finally spoke him he was really mean over the phone and FINALLY said he had dumped me. Why couldn't he have told me this three months earlier? As a result of this, I entered into a depression that lasted nearly two years."

Angie goes on to describe how, after recovering from her depression, she met the man who would become her husband and they moved back to the west coast.

"We ran out of money, couldn't find work and spent three months in a sleazy homeless shelter. Eventually we went back to Indiana. We got married and had two children. Things have improved for me, but now it is my nasty mother-in-law who keeps putting me down. I am trying to ignore it, but it is difficult to feel good about myself and my life while hearing these negative comments."

One important factor that sets people up for codependency isn't their relationship with others but their relationship with themselves. Not assuming false roles, accepting yourself for what and who you are, is an essential task in becoming an independent being. It is also imperative not to set yourself the task of being a lifeline for a needy partner or friend, but to assist that person in getting the professional help he or she needs.

◀ 7 ▶

Top 40 Countdown
to Losing Yourself:
Beneath the Cotton Candy Lyrics,
the Bitter Aftertaste

I grew up a self-proclaimed head banger, singing along to some pretty rough music. The lyrics and rhythm of my favorite bands were far from docile. With pounding beats and harrowing guitar riffs, it didn't matter what the song was about or what the words were. Lyrics from Guns-n-Roses rolled right off my tongue without stopping in my head for dissection. A few choice lyrics come to mind from their *Appetite for Destruction* album:

"It's So Easy"

> *Turn around bitch I got a use for you,*
> *besides you ain't got nothin' better to do,*
> *and I'm bored.*

"Rocket Queen"

> *I've got a tongue like a razor,*
> *a sweet switchblade knife*
> *and I can do you favors*
> *but then you'll do whatever I like.*

I rode around with my friends, screaming at the top of my lungs, never stopping to analyze what was coming out of my mouth. To be quite honest, I'm still stuck in the '80s and have a book full of CDs with nothing but, including these very songs. I rock away, pretending I'm still young, but I catch myself occasionally when I'm singing, realizing in shock what I've just bellowed out in the privacy of my car. Certain CDs I won't play in the presence of my sons, who are right at the age I was when I started to listening to these very same bands.

As bad as lyrics were twenty years ago, the majority of today's popular music showcases maximum physical and sexual violence against women without retribution of any kind. Songs are available now like they weren't then—through MTV, BET and the Internet. If that weren't enough, they are on every radio countdown several times a week. It's not just rock and roll, but rap and even pop as well. Songs portray violent misogynistic messages aimed at preserving male dominance and female subjugation and many youths today approach their relationships with the opposite sex mimicking the attitudes of the rock or rap entertainer.

Researchers have found that such portrayals of women as victims of violence or as sexual objects may influence how women are viewed and treated in society. Listening to the remix of Usher's "Confessions," I am truly sickened by not only what I hear, but knowing that children are singing right along. These lyrics have been edited on some radio versions, but not all, and are still available for download on the Internet:

> *Pray that she abort that*
> *If she's talkin' 'bout keepin' it,*
> *One hit to the stomach,*
> *She's leakin' it.*

The "she" in the lyrics is referring not to the man's girlfriend, but his girl "on the side," whom in the song he swears off in an attempt to get to keep his girlfriend. With Usher's popularity (his songs are seven, eight and thirteen in this week's top forty), how is this influencing today's youth? Throngs of screaming girls await him wherever he may be even though he sings of abusing the ones stupid enough to get pregnant by him. Even though he brags of cheating on his girlfriend. And while they are just lyrics and not his real life, the children listening take his word as Scripture. They become inured to ideas of sexual objectification, depictions of violence against women and the frequent association of violence with sexuality.

The popular Music Television (MTV) channel has been found to show an average of eighteen instances of aggression per hour of air time. Over one-third of these instances involve sexual violence against women. In a recent study, researchers found that college-age men who are exposed to a significant amount of violence and misogyny in music videos may actually become more likely to commit rape due to the desensitization that comes with repeated viewings of these acts. Rape and the subjugation of women are themes that have become prevalent in popular music of the past decade or more. An example of this is Cannibal Corpse's song "Stripped, Raped, and Strangled," the title of which is enough to suggest a theme of violence.[1] When they are constantly hearing this type of message and seeing these images of violence and objectification of women, how can we expect our boys to treat girls?

The defining moment when I realized that this would be a chapter in my book was when a group of my first grade girls ran up to me at recess. As they begged me to watch their dance, they gathered in a circle. I was overcome by memories of "Ring around the Rosie" and "Miss Mary Mack," only to find myself in the Twilight Zone. Holding hands, turning and twisting about the circle, each girl would take a turn "dancing" in the middle. By dancing I mean gyrating and "popping," which means getting down real low, lower than I could get with my old joints, and grinding the air as though it was a man. Lewd movements that they learned watching MTV, sexual gestures, everything I saw sickened me. The girls were too young to know how provocative their dances were and were blissfully ignorant of the leering boys surrounding them. If that wasn't disgusting enough, the lyrics they were rapping made me sick deep down inside. These children had trouble learning how to spell ten words a week and their ABCs, but they knew this song by heart, word for word.

I was in shock. My sweet little girls, who should be princesses, were singing about being used by men and enjoying it, singing about selling your body to pay your bills. And singers like Lil' Kim are the role models of these girls and their mothers. Lil' Kim, who struts about wearing nothing but tassels and a mini-skirt on award shows and magazine covers. I looked at my girls and wondered how many of them will be abused and pregnant before they hit high school.

Later that day I spoke to my boys and girls separately and tried to impart a little wisdom about the strengths they held, not to use or be used by anyone. They had no clue what I meant; it was too abstract. But I can only hope one day they'll recall it when the time is right. That time will come, without a doubt.

While research has shown that men who habitually listen to rap, heavy metal and other music with violent or misogynistic lyrics tend to have more negative attitudes towards women than men who listen to other types of music, not everyone who listens to this music will become an abuser or be abused.[2] Just like codependency, it takes a variety of factors to create situations like these. Children raised in homes where parents speak with them often, share and are open to questions in a safe and healthy environment will likely not be drawn in. But the children in my class, as well as millions like them across the country, have no role models. The majority of my students have missing parents, in jail or dead, and are living with grandmothers or great-grandmothers who can barely walk. Their only meal of the day is lunch at the cafeteria and most don't want to leave school at three o'clock. Their homes have no electricity or running water and they hang out on the streets till late at night, watching the older kids, listening to the music and seeing how they treat each other. What will become of them when their role models aren't a strong, dedicated mother and father, but are rappers who are only concerned with selling records?

Lyrics are part of the wallpaper of our lives, available in many resources throughout the day and night. We hear the same lyrics over and over again, in shops, bars, clubs, in our cars, on our walkmans. Through repeated listening, lyrics enter our consciousness and make the language and ideas expressed in them seem familiar and comfortable. The constant barrage of these lyrics helps abusers to feel okay about what they're doing and the abused to feel that this is the norm.

One of the highest paid artists today is Eminem, whose violent lyrics are well known and controversial. However, the controversy among adults only serves to market his music further. This is what our children listen to and sing along with on the Rick Dee's Weekly Top 40 on Sunday evenings and MTV's Total Request Live:

"Stan"

> *Hey Slim, that's my girlfriend screamin' in the trunk,*
> *but I didn't slit her throat, I just tied her up, see I ain't*
> *like you.*

"Kim"

> *Come on we're going for a ride bitch... sit up front...*
> *We'll be right back, well I will, you'll be in the trunk.*

"Murder Murder"

> *You barely heard a word as she choked,*
> *It wasn't nuttin' for her to be smoked,*
> *But I slammed her on her back 'til her vertebrae broke.*

These horrific lyrics are sung by blacks and whites, preteens, teens and adults throughout the United States and abroad. My own children probably know them, if I'm quite honest. I banned them from listening to this type of music, but I can't be with them every minute of the day. I only hope that I've taught them to respect and value women and that they carry my words in their heads forever.

While boys are looking up to Eminem, emulating and mimicking him, girls want to be Lil' Kim and Britney Spears. While Britney's lyrics aren't as overtly degrading to women as Lil' Kim's, the sexual objectification, submissive attitudes and needy behavior are rampant. "Baby One More Time" and "Everytime" portray women as less than whole without men, perpetuating codependency on a daily basis. To make the impact even worse for young children, who soak up impressions and information like sponges, the video for "Everytime" shows Britney slitting her wrists over her man, willing to die for his love.

"Baby One More Time"

> *When I'm not with you I lose my mind*
> *Give me a sign*
> *Hit me baby one more time.*

"Everytime"

> *Everytime I try to fly*
> *I fall without my wings*
> *I feel so small*
> *I guess I need you baby.*

As much as I hate to admit it, I listen to this music too; put any words to a cool beat and melody, throw in a half-dressed anorexic diva or a gun-toting foulmouthed rap/rock mogul, and that's the recipe for a megahit. The results? Countless dollars for the industry, lost souls on the streets. Our culture shows a shocking acceptance of violence against and ill-usage of women in the entertainment industry. With catchy rhythms and melodies, children are sucked in, hearing without listening, singing without comprehension. They are deadened to violence against women by men. Despite debate on the appropriateness of lyrics, millions of albums are sold to kids from ages fourteen to twenty-four. Number one songs are played hourly on popular radio stations and music video television, inundating youth with messages of female objectification and physical violence, keeping women at a disadvantage in our society.

◀ 8 ▶

The Media–Entertaining Our Minds, Destroying Our Psyches

In spite of professional advice and keen insight, I still struggle with my self-image. I don't hear compliments; insults echo ad infinitum in my head, reverberating endlessly lest I forget how "imperfect" I am. Remembering what I looked like when I was a teenager, I can't believe how unhappy I was back then. The old Bekah was indeed pretty. Yet somehow I know that even if I was her again, I'd still not be satisfied. Now, however, I am more at peace with my body.

At the height of my "best figure" days, I was at the lowest of my self-concept. I'd just entered basic training in the Air Force and was fit and trim with voluptuous curves in all the right places. Not an ounce of fat, nary a dimpled thigh to be found. My grandma even measured me, a perfect 36-24-36. I was blind to the good, drawn to the flaws. My nose was monstrous, that huge bump of a legacy. My brown eyes were too brown, my lower lip too big, my shoulders too narrow. My hair too thick, cheekbones non-existent, smile lopsided, butt too wide, boobs heavy and awkward. I look back at that girl in the picture and think how beautiful she was. Who or what made her so blind to that beauty?

I hit rock bottom of my vanity spiral one morning on the way to the mess hall. In basic training, if your eyes are less than perfect you have to wear what they call birth control glasses, so named because no one will want to give you a second look in them. I had true coke bottles, rimmed by thick brown frames, which accented my plain brown eyes so well. Rather than wear them, I violated the no-contact rules, risking the wrath of one of my instructors daily. At 4 AM each day, when the other girls were making their "bounce a quarter off my sheets" beds, I was racing to stick my contacts in at the water fountain, the ice water burning my corneas for hours afterward. It was worth it. There was a flight of boys next door and I was being courted by no less than three of them. I thought they'd ditch me for sure if they knew I wasn't perfect, and what better to ruin their perception of me than a pair of magnifying glasses bringing attention to my enormous honker?

One morning, as I barreled down the hallway toward the fountain, I ran smack dab into the instructor, guarding my most prized hideout. Surely she couldn't know what I'd been doing. I pressed on, feigning a killer thirst. As I choked down the water, I felt her glaring at me, never backing down an inch. I knew then that it would be geek Rebekah for the day and maybe the rest to come. My social life was being sucked down the drain before my very eyes. I marched back to my quarters and tightened my sheets, the instructor breathing down my neck all the while.

As we marched in formation, I felt like my glasses were a magnet for jeers and stares. Looking back, I was a blithering idiot. No one cared; no one noticed. I was not the center of everyone's universe, only my own. The instructor I'd had a problem with held the idea that if we ran to breakfast and each meal thereafter, it would make us stronger women. Didn't work for me. I was shorter than most of the girls and had to push myself harder to keep up with the longer legs of the rest of the flight. I've never been very coordinated so keeping left right left right going while struggling to maintain the pace of the others took all the concentration I could muster.

In the distance I could hear the strains of young men shouting out cadence on their way back to the barracks. I knew that it was the group of young men who were our counterparts in training and that my three suitors would be on the watch for me. Sitting alone in church later that day, without a boy next to me, would certainly lead to my untimely demise. Church dating was as good as it could get in basic training. Sitting in God's house was the only event that was an option out there, and even the die-hard atheists managed to find a seat in the pew just to have an hour of freedom. And if you had a good-looking cadet sitting next to you, well, that was closer to Heaven than the preacher could ever get you.

As they marched closer, I knew the glasses had to go. They were the only thing that stood between me and the love of my life, whoever that was. I yanked them off and stuffed them in my pocket at the last second before they pulled neck and neck with us. Breaking formation, I turned a flirtatious smile upon the group, which I couldn't see because I'm practically blind without the aid of my glasses. As I grinned lasciviously at the blur of hot young soldiers, I forgot to pace myself... right left right left keep up with the group right left right left a little faster... smiling and focusing and jogging proved to be too much for my two left feet. In one quick moment, which lasted a lifetime, I went from jogging to being crushed into the ground, gravel staving its way into my cheeks and mouth and hands. A virtual domino rally was taking place about me, with all the girls in their combat boots kicking me as they fell, my fat ass cushioning their plummets. And the only thing I could think of at the bottom of that pile, blood already burning my eyes, was if I'd have any scars, which would keep me from church this morning and my hour with a boy.

I wonder how I got this way. I wonder how I could be blind to how pretty I was, how the mirror could be so distorted. Reading my *People* magazine, the cover with Mary Kate and Ashley Olsen shouting out dysfunctionality while insinuating perfection, I see that the media is a blueprint for how women today must look. Mary Kate's too thin, deathly skinny (but isn't she beautiful) and losing weight at a dangerous speed (but she looks great in that Prada dress) and, my, you can count her ribs and her cheekbones are jutting out (just type in key word "pro-ana" on the web). The media—movies, commercials, music videos, television and magazines—are the most pervasive communicators of culture, desirable yet unattainable perfection, which leads to low self-esteem, eating disorders, unhealthy body image and increased acceptance of violence against women. The constant feeling of falling short of one's ideals or expectations can be extremely detrimental to building healthy self-esteem.[1] The media is a profit-seeking industry and sadly, whether right or wrong, stereotypes sell. Would we really buy *People*'s fifty most beautiful if they catalogued women with wrinkles, saddlebags and birth control glasses?

The facts regarding media images of feminine ideals and the effects these ideals have on girls' and women's perceptions of themselves are disturbing. Here are some sample statistics:[2]

▶ Nearly half of all girls in the U.S. between the ages of eleven and thirteen feel that they are overweight.

▶ In a survey of thirteen-year-old girls, 80 percent admitted to dieting or other measures in attempts to lose weight.

▶ Among adolescents, anorexia nervosa is the third most common chronic illness.

▶ Eating disorders are most prevalent in the twelve to twenty-five age group, which accounts for 95 percent of all eating disorders diagnosed.

▶ Among women aged eighteen to twenty-four, 25 percent rely on bingeing and purging behaviors to help maintain weight.

An expert researcher, Adrienne Ressler, M.S., C.S.W., is a body image specialist for the Renfrew Center, a residential facility for women with eating disorders. In a recent study on how everyday toys affect girls' self-concepts and self-esteem, Ressler found that a number of toys on the market that are specifically aimed at girls could be harmful to their self-esteem. Many of the popular games for girls focus on dating, shopping and physical appearances. The winner is the girl who is most popular with the boys, best dressed or prettiest. According to Ressler, "The message that kids are getting at an early age from these toys is that this is what women and girls do best."

Ninety percent of the toys and dolls slanted for girls have zoned in on three areas: shopping, beauty and dating, according to their survey. Ressler asks why malls have few book and museum shops and suggests better choices, including racially and physically diverse dolls. Her suggestions hinge on assessing a child's natural tendencies, talents and inclination.[3] Some tips for doing this:

- ▶ Children's advertising is manipulative. Don't give them everything they want.
- ▶ Let your child choose imaginative toys without your control. Guide, don't order them.
- ▶ Take time to consider purchases. When you choose a toy, consider whether it will stimulate growth, creativity and imagination.
- ▶ Communicate with your child about why he or she likes a certain toy *before*, not after you buy it.

As they move from childhood to adolescence, both girls and boys begin to redefine themselves, looking to many sources for guidance throughout this process. From an early age girls are active participants in the media community, watching over twenty hours of television a week, seeing 20,000 advertisements a year, listening to radio and CDs, watching music videos, reading fashion magazines and newspapers and playing video games. Researchers have suggested that the cumulative impact of this media may be one of the most influential forces in the adolescent community.

Not only are the physical characteristics of women being massaged and manipulated in the media, but the lifestyles are as well. Women are most often portrayed in the context of relationships on TV and in the movies. Men, on the other hand, are most often seen in the context of careers, intelligent and strong-minded.

Childrennow.org research has shown that the media plays a powerful role in shaping children's beliefs, attitudes and perceptions. Among their research findings are that women date more often than men do in a range of media: 23 percent of women on television shows were dating, compared to 17 percent of men. In movies 27 percent of women and 16 percent of men were dating. Commercials depicted 9 percent of women and only 4 percent of men dating. Men's concentration are scenes on the job, where 41 percent of men are shown compared to 28 percent of women. In movies it jumps to 60 percent of men and 35 percent of women. Commercials reflect this trend as well, with 17 percent of men and 9 percent of women shown in job-related contexts.[4]

A big motivation for women is the desire for a romantic liaison. Thirty-two percent of women on television are portrayed in this situation, 35 percent in movies. Men only score about 20 percent in both of these categories. Success on the job, according to TV portrayals, motivates 32 percent of men, but only 24 percent of women. In movies there is over a 20 percent differential when showing men's motivation for career aspiration as compared to women. Another media form, magazines, strengthens this message about dating being the be all and end all for women: a full 35 percent of articles in women's magazines focus on dating and relationships.[4]

As a result of mass conformity to female stereotypes, education and careers have faltered for women in comparison to men. By the end of the 1990s, although there were more women in the college setting and entering "male" professions, there remained a huge gap in salary between male and female counterparts. Although we've all heard that teachers and parents push boys into math, science and business fields and girls into teaching and nursing, it was never quite as alarming to me as it was when I was researching this book and laid my eyes on the results of a study by the National Center for Education Statistics. According to the study that I saw, the majority of students in fields such as business, computers, engineering, law, mathematics, medicine and dentistry were male, while the majority of students in education, literature, foreign language, health sciences, nursing and social sciences were female.[5] Not only does this reflect the types of jobs that are considered suited to traditional male and female roles, but it also reflects the huge gap in earning potential for men and women, as many of the fields dominated by male students, such as law, medicine and engineering, are much more lucrative than those with a majority of female students.

Magazines and variety news shows in 2004 were harping on Mary Kate Olsen and others for becoming anorexic, but top magazines showcase only the thinnest women, few having more curves than a twelve-year-old boy. Top female actresses are stick thin, because that is the ideal in today's society. While men are accepted in various ages, shapes and sizes, women are not allowed that variance. The message sent is, Thin is in! Don't be anorexic, that's bad, but get as close as you can without dying!!! These are the images our girls see at the checkouts and newsstands. If a pimple or a wrinkle mars the perfection, these icons have plastic surgery or Botox. Their pictures make other young girls feel inadequate. An article on Paris Hilton says she gets her baby blues through contacts, her long hair through extensions and straightens out her frizz with a professional blow dry every time it's washed. The rate at which such young celebrities must maintain perfection, the stress of being "on" all the time, must be horrendous. Our society's customs made Mary Kate into an anorexic. We should be ashamed.

One of the worst purveyors of female stereotyping is the rock/rap video. Women are portrayed as sexual objects, often wearing little more than a string bikini, undulating for the pleasure of the males in the video. The men move from woman to woman, gyrating, using, abusing before moving on to the next. And according to the storyline, the women stand for it, accepting them back, moving on to the next man in line. According to behavioral and cognitive-developmental psychologists, ideas about gender behavior and appearance develop from repetitive exposure and learned behavior acquired through continued experience and interaction with the outside environment. Typical teenagers spend more time watching television shows and will remember more of what they see there than what they learn at school, and will take their cues on gender expectations through what they see their role models doing.

I'm still stuck on these poor young girls in the entertainment industry. Many of these women exercise five and six hours a day, existing on greens and water. They have surgeries and botox, whatever it takes to maintain their images—their paychecks. These role models, thrust to the top like bullets, speed down toward their deaths. Britney Spears, hailed as a pop goddess, is pictured in a magazine and on the web with a close-up on her backside, highlighting a dimple. An unflattering picture showing her six-pack abs a little out of shape shouts out "Pregnancy?" "Is Britney letting herself go?" "Fab to Flab!" And the following week, the exact same girl is on the best-dressed page, looking sleek and svelte in her designer gown. This young girl, beautiful and thin already, is unable to let her guard down for a moment without the media slamming her. The media glorifies their perfection, crushes them for the flaws.

How do we stop this vicious cycle? Become a little more comfortable in your own skin. Despite the setbacks—the beautiful girls at the pool making us feel less than worthy, goddesses on the magazine pages showing you what you can be if you starve yourself, girls with impossible Barbie dimensions frolicking about on MTV, garnering the attention of all the men—strive to celebrate your uniqueness. Most of all, let us help our children to break out, to have peace in themselves. The Media Awareness Network offers a tip list on talking to kids about gender stereotypes. Among the things they suggest are:[6]

> Speak to children about stereotypes and explain how these simplified portrayals do not reflect real people and may even be hurtful. Discuss stereotypes that appear in books or television shows to which your children are exposed. Emphasize characters that break free of the stereotypical mold.

> Analyze male and female stereotypes in advertising and other media and explain to children that they need not be limited to the prescribed roles. Let them know that it is perfectly normal and acceptable for girls to be aggressive and physically active and for boys to be quiet or artistic.

> Encourage children to question portrayals they see in the media. Do these images resemble people they know in real life? In what different ways are men and women shown to be "good" or worthwhile? What issues concern these characters? Are the issues the same or different for men and women? Do these reflect the concerns of real people?

> Find and identify a stereotypical man and woman in advertising or other media and point out the characteristics that each is supposed to possess. Talk to your children about how these images make us view men and women and how they can be limiting for both.

▶ Video games can be an unexpected source of gender stereotypes. There are distinctly different types of games for girls and boys. Ask your children to think about these games. In games for girls, the focus is often on make-up or fashion, while boys' games tend to focus on action, violence and aggression. Why do they think these divisions are made?

▶ Be sure to discuss popular music, which is so pervasive in our culture. What tactics do male and female artists use to market their music? Do they differ significantly? How are men and women portrayed in songs and music videos?

▶ Seek out and expose your children to non-traditional characters of both sexes. Emphasize the positive examples provided by these role models and encourage your children to follow in their footsteps rather simple accepting stereotypical roles.

Changing these stereotypes will be a long, uphill battle. Celebrities like Oprah Winfrey have their weight loss and gain chronicled daily. Oprah, in my opinion, is a no-holds-barred strong female role model and yet society brings her down with every inch and pound she gains. Women in television and movie roles that are portrayed as dominant and powerful are seen as simultaneously beautiful and sexy, thin with huge breasts. Barbie all over again. Yet there are a few female leads that mirror the true American woman, women like Kirstie Alley, Elizabeth Edwards and even supersized models who are increasing in popularity. Commit yourself to teaching your children to love themselves and to treat others with respect regardless of their appearance. If you do, then we will grow in maturity and our next generation may be a little better, a little stronger and a lot smarter.

Part
◀ 3 ▶

Cyber Codependency–
Relationship
Addiction Made Easy

◀ 9 ▶

Love without Leaving Your Armchair:
Internet Users and Their Confessions

Surfing on the web is a whole new reality or pseudo reality, which sucks in many types of people, young and old, men and women. In my research I have found, though, that the majority of users trapped by Internet relationship addiction are those with low self-concepts, codependency and dysfunctional familial and relationship history. The reality of the web is that "operators" can do the same smooth talking they'd do in bars, but now with a wife, husband, boy- or girlfriend or kids in the very same room. Men can pretend to be women, women can have their ideal body image and children can profess to be adults. You can be wearing stilettos or bunny slippers, lace or wool. It's convenient and who knows the difference? Why do people lie to people they'll never meet? Because they think others won't want to pass the time of day with them if they're not perfect? So true. It's the surfers' chance to be just that, perfect, and no one will know the difference. They can create an online image of themselves that's in line with society's concept of a "10." And others believe that lie because they want to think that they're conversing with perfection.

In my own circle of friends there have been one-night stands, long term relationships gone bad and even marriages with Internet users. In almost all the cases, both sides of the duos misrepresented themselves, leading to the ultimate demise of the relationships. The other day a friend of a friend told me that the wife of thirty-five years of a nice gentlemen who works at the local laundry left him for a man she met on the Internet. The wife, who'd been corresponding with this man online for a year, flew off to the Bahamas dreaming of living happily ever after. Sadly, the picture she'd emailed to her beloved was that of a model and when the man saw her at the airport, he left her there, with no money and no return ticket. She called her husband begging him to forgive and send her a ticket. He, obviously codependent, Western Unioned her the money. I pray that she learns her lesson.

I feel strongly that Internet addiction and the struggle with negative self-concept through societal stereotyping go hand in hand. The feeling of being wanted, needed, loved, whether in life or virtual reality, is something we all crave. Those who don't feel worthy enough to get those things in the outside world fall prey to the traps available online. Lying and accepting lies as truths are part of the pattern. Budding codependents fall in love with words, when often the words mean nothing.

Bart, one man who spoke to me, is young and on the make, trying to find someone to meet him for a one-night stand. Early Friday evenings he is online chatting with up to six or seven women at a time. Instead of having personal conversations, he cuts and pastes the same lines and responses over and over to the various women and they invariably fall for it. He never spends a Friday night alone and never calls the women the next day. And the ruse begins again on Saturday night. Though it is easy to blame Bart, I can't attribute fault to him alone. I've spoken to many women who mistake attention for affection, sex for love. In a day where strong relationships are rare, members of both sexes—but again, especially women—settle for one-night stands to feel loved.

Persons addicted to the Internet often have problems with other addictions as well: gambling, drugs, relationship, drinking and eating disorders—any behavior that has mood-altering effects can become an addiction by eliciting neurochemical changes that occur as the pleasurable behavior occurs. Chemical changes bring about a temporary feeling of pleasure, which is likely to be repeated, reinforcing the addictive cycle. They may feel that the Internet is a "safe" outlet... no physical damages or financial destruction, but that isn't always the case. The extended use of the Internet and its traps lead to interference with work, family life, school, relationships, etc. Often the shame and guilt after Internet encounters become real life encounters leads to physical symptoms or anxiety and ulcers, not to mention sexually transmitted diseases. If a surfer looking for sex lies about his or her looks and income, why would he or she tell you about that raging case of herpes?

Shelly tells us about the ordeal of finding out her partner was seeking company on the Internet:

"My husband and I live in Maryland. We got married about five years ago. We were truly best friends, soul mates and exact mirror images of each other. He was the male me, and I was the female him. Our relationship seemed wonderful, because we didn't fight about anything; every 'disagreement' was so petty that we overcame it quickly. We enjoyed playing games on Internet gaming sites. He built a computer for my thirteen-year-old son and he had ours in the other room. We would play Scrabble and Monopoly against each other in opposite rooms, which was really fun. About a year and a half after we married, he had found a 'friend' in one gaming site who was having problems in her relationship. He was giving her examples of how he treated me like a queen and how great our relationship was. He kept this 'friendship' a secret from me, and would only talk to this person when I was at work. I asked him numerous times if he was cheating on me because his actions were indicating that he was. He was very distant, defensive, and he was always complaining about something in our marriage (lack of money, inability to communicate, my 'controlling' nature). I had not noticed any of these supposed problems. My husband even took himself off all of his anti-depressant medication because he 'wanted to be totally in control of himself and his actions.' Well, it turns out that his 'friend' was from Spain, was about twelve years older than him, and has several children. I found e-mails sent back and forth between them saying, 'I'm so lucky to have found the love of my life. I love you...' Next he said he looked up careers in Spain for me and that I could make much more money there and advance quickly in my field. He also claimed to have researched the education system in Spain and tried to persuade me that it would be an advantage to my son. He actually had me believing him and my mind was open to the possibilities. Well, unfortunately, this all happened around tax refund time. To sum this up, he took half our tax check (he didn't want to leave me with absolutely nothing—how nice of him). He said he was going to Spain with or without me. The day he left, he was all dressed up in a new suit and tie. He 'wanted to look professional' for his new start. He called me from the airport and said, 'This isn't going to work. I don't think I'm coming back. I'll HAVE to make it work out there somehow.' His plane ticket was round trip so I suspected he would be back at some point. He only had a couple thousand dollars.

"I was so hurt that I couldn't eat or sleep. All I could do was cry. Even though my husband did this to me, I still cared about his well-being. He was in a foreign country where he didn't know anyone, didn't have a good grasp of the language, didn't know where he was going or how to get there. I was more or less scared for him and there was nothing I could do because I didn't know how to contact him to make sure he was okay. Well, about four days after he left, he called me. He had bought a 'pay-by-minute' cell phone. I asked him if he was done being immature and if he was ready to come home to work this out. He said he was so scared, he found a hotel room, things didn't work out for the job search, he was running out of money, and he missed me and wanted to come home.

"I waited for his return flight date and picked him up at the airport. I couldn't help noticing that he had a Spanish accent already, and he had only been there two weeks. Well, when we got home from the airport, there was a message on my answering machine from a woman (with a Spanish accent) who said, 'Mrs. W****, I think you should ask your husband where he's been for the last two weeks and whose bed he's been sleeping in.' I was shocked!!!! He told me that he met up with that woman from the Internet and she showed him around a little... but that was it. I didn't believe him so I said, 'Let's call her.' We called her (I was on one phone and he was on another) and I got all my answers and confirmations. My husband was literally sick, crying and vomiting because I had caught him in a serious lie. We were on the phone for over an hour. After he finally came clean, I let him stay in the house but in separate rooms. We talked about everything to what she looked like (nasty and old) to how many times they had sex, to his thoughts about what he did to me. We agreed to work it out with counseling, church, and support from our family and friends. Things did improve for about a year and a half. Then... just recently, he started acting strangely again. I asked him if everything was okay, and he said, 'Yes.' He was playing a new game an awful lot on this other gaming site we had been a part of and getting awfully flirtatious. I occasionally snooped in the computer (as I had every right to do) but I couldn't find anything. Either he was very, very sneaky and had a hidden program to cover his tracks, or he really wasn't doing anything wrong. This went on for a couple of months. He eventually said that he got tired of me sneaking around to check up on him, looking over his shoulder when he was in the gaming room, looking through the cookies and temporary Internet files. I really didn't find anything, so I felt like a fool. I was happy that I didn't find anything.

"The truth was, he just gave up and said, 'F*** it, if she wants to find something, I'll give her something to find.' He got a voice mail on his cell phone, a woman's voice saying, 'Hi baby, I know you can't answer your phone right now...' (Click).... He deleted the message and the phone number. When I questioned him about it, he blew up, packed his things and moved to his parents' house. Guess what? This time the woman was from Florida, six years older with three kids. At least this time he stayed in his own country!!! He got very close to this woman in just a matter of weeks. It wasn't long before he told me that she was coming here with two of her three children to find a job, because he loved her and she loved him. The plan was that they were going to find a place together and live happily ever after. He had no idea what she looked like, but he sent her pictures of him. One photo was of him in his tuxedo AT OUR WEDDING. I was crushed once again. When he did this before, running off to Spain, I completely blew up at him. This time, I just let him go. He was staying with his parents just a few miles away. We exchanged bitter e-mails and instant messages and there were three-way phone calls with the woman in Florida. I tried to warn her about what he had done to me only a year before. I said that he had to suffer from some type of mental illness, to continue to display this kind of addiction. That didn't stop her from coming to see him.

"She stayed only a few days over a long weekend. I had somewhat given up the fight for him so I decided that I would go out with one of our mutual friends. I had a great time, but I still was keeping my eye open in case we accidentally bumped into my husband and his new girlfriend. When my date and I came back to my apartment, things started to get rather steamy, but they didn't go as far as they could have. I still had respect for myself as a woman, a mother and a wife. Two wrongs don't make a right. I sent an email to my husband stating that I had moved on, went out with 'our friend,' gave him some of the details of our date and thanked him for making me open my eyes.

"My husband and I kept in touch with each other and our bitterness was slowly subsiding. Then he said he realized where he belonged... with me. He really understood that we were best friends and he didn't want to lose that. He said he was sorry for hurting my son and me again. He was willing to give our marriage one final chance if I was willing to also. Well, I also have a disease called 'codependency,' so I agreed that we would work it out. He put all his possessions in storage, including his computer. He had a few conditions before we would try to work it out. We would go to counseling (more than twice this time), we would get our cell phone numbers changed, get our email addresses and screen names changed, change our home phone number, and start all over again... from scratch. He would stay at his parent's house and we would 'date,' exclusively. We would start off slowly again, and get our sparks back. I am still keeping my guard up because I don't want to get hurt again. The only thing that has come between us in our marriage is the Internet. That's it! This is all new to me and I don't know how to deal with it. I know it's an addiction and there's got to be some way to treat it."

Cassandra was herself an Internet surfer and talks from the opposite perspective.

"I was a single mom, living in a very small town, with virtually no form of recreation (no YWCA, no malls, movie theaters, etc.). The Internet became my 'link to the world.' Like so many people in this situation, the first thing I would do in the morning was log on, so I could carry on conversations with instant messaging or visit my favorite chat room. I had several online relationships. The trouble was, I was honest to a fault, but the men involved (I later found out) were always much older, married, and had children. It was all just a game to them, a salve for their ego. Talk about feeling like you've wasted your life! My son and my family begged me to spend more time with them, and less time online... but the people I met online were my FRIENDS and I felt that they understood me. Boy, was I in deep! I got married a few months ago. Luckily, we spend virtually NO time on the computer at home now, unless we need it for research. After having been away from the chat sites for so long, I decided to revisit them, out of morbid curiosity, I guess. I never thought I'd find the same old people, but I did. Three years later, there they were, still chatting, still lying. I'm so glad I'm no longer one of them. It wasn't easy to break this habit. At times, I felt almost physical withdrawal symptoms. But believe me, it's worth it. Living on the Internet is not living at all, regardless of what someone tries to tell you. Please don't be naïve like me and fall for the lies people tell you online. I'd be more than happy to correspond with anyone needing support for this growing problem."

Surfers come in all ages, occupations and both sexes. Perry is another surfer who admits he's addicted to the Internet:

"My problem started two years ago when my ex-wife bought me a computer. I was unemployed at the time and spent twelve to sixteen hours a day on the net. My wife got fed up and gave me a choice between her and the internet. I picked the net. It has gotten worse now. I live for the net. I can't wait to get home at lunch to go online and when I get home at night I go online. My kids hate that I never seem to have time for them anymore. I had the most beautiful girlfriend whom I met online and we decided to meet in person.

She visited me for ten days before she broke up with me because of the net. My life has become a total wreck. I don't sleep well at night, I don't eat right and on weekends all I want to do is go online. I need help and I am scared, because my life is spinning out of control. I am setting up counseling, but I'm not sure how to kick the addiction."

Derek shares a similar story of Internet addiction and its consequences:

"When I was working at a place in the mid-nineties that let employees use the company Internet connection to surf the web, I thought to myself, 'This is a new thing and I'm going to learn it.' I was already good with computers, but the net was a new thing. At one point my growing addiction got so bad that I actually made a copy of the keys to the building that the computer was in so I could sneak in there at night and use the machine. One night I was on the net for ten hours straight! Obviously with the increasing phone bill the company knew something was up and moved the computer away from the building and started charging people for using it. By that time I had left the company and to fuel my addiction I started going to my dad's house to try and convince him that he needed a computer. Eventually he did buy one and I went to his house all the time to use it. I registered a dotcom, which was a good excuse to use my dad's machine so I could update my site, but I would spend hours on it doing nothing but general surfing. As soon as I was finished surfing I would quickly say goodbye to my dad and leave without even having a chat with him about anything else I had been doing in my life at that time. Next I bought a computer for my own home and started using it all the time until I received a huge phone bill and I knew I had to cut down. But soon I stumbled across 'free internet' and that was it! I would arrive home from work and switch my computer on and stay on it until 10 PM. On Fridays I would stay on the computer until the early hours of the morning and then get up at 6 AM on Saturday and Sunday so I could spend all day on the net. At that point I did not want to go to social evenings with family and friends, because my addiction was so bad. I also had a partner who put up with a whole lot. There were many rows about the time I spent on the Internet and it started to create problems between us. For a while we came to a compromise whereby I would only go on the net at the weekends, but it soon spiraled back into me using on weekdays as well. I have now registered another dotcom and am working hard on that. I have also managed to cut down my Internet usage to a couple of days a week and sometimes on the weekend or when my partner is working and I am at home. I still have problems with not going on the net. I sometimes get anxious because I think I might be missing something or there might be an important email for me to answer.

"I tell myself there isn't anything I am missing and the emails can wait until another day, but it's very hard. I have a wonderful job and a wonderful partner, but it is very difficult to keep off the net. I suppose a good thing has happened at work, where they have given me full net access to use during lunchtimes. Now I can get my fill at work and I don't have to go on my machine at home in the evenings as much. It is getting better and I am not as addicted as I used to be a few years ago, but I still need to cut down. I suppose it must be like smoking or drinking: you can't cut it out straight away, but if you do it slowly it is manageable. Not only that, but if you have a partner, being addicted to the net puts a huge strain on your relationship. I've been lucky, but there were some occasions when we very nearly split up. Internet addiction is a real thing and is becoming increasingly common."

Terry is young, attractive and successful, but also addicted to the net.

"I bought my first computer two years ago, and I have been hooked ever since. Everything in my life has changed as a result of this addiction. When I wake up in the morning, the first thing I do is turn on is the computer. I do not get coffee, dress, or even say good morning to my daughters. I log in and just surf—I do not accomplish anything. I am taking courses in computer programming and I am falling behind. It is ironic: I am falling behind on what I am addicted to in the first place.

"My job performance has suffered; I do not visit or spend time with my friends or family. When I go out to work or run errands all I ever think about is logging on again. I have real difficulty thinking about anything else. I try getting the thoughts out of my head, but I am having progressively worsening symptoms of withdrawal. These symptoms include sweats, obsessive thoughts, shaking, 'butterflies' (the kind you get when you anticipate something you want), and even anger.

"When I log in, I get a euphoria like I am the queen of the world and in full control. I know I can be anybody I want to be, do anything I want to do, and say whatever I want to say without consequence. I surf aimlessly, chat, play with applications, play a game, download music, and read information. I love the endless information at my fingertips. I read about the news, jokes, facts and other stuff that does not pertain to my life or real life whatsoever. This information does not help for school, yet I love every second that I spend on my computer reading it. Meanwhile, my kids are being neglected, the housework is not getting done and I am not spending time with friends, God, and most of all, my family. I know this in the back of my head when I am surfing the net, but I do not care while I am getting my 'fix.' After I get my 'fix' the cycle is completed: I feel guilty, paranoid, depressed, and angry and am very apologetic. I have told my family before I would stop, but now they do not believe me... and why should they? I do not keep my promises. I even lie because of the computer. My life is in a downward spiral and I am afraid that I cannot help myself. I know I need help, and I am addicted to the computer."

Stephen, a mature man, stumbled innocently, he says, into a chat room and became enamored.

"My wife and I have been married for nineteen years, and until six months ago, we had a very good relationship. I stumbled innocently into a job-related chat room, on a large Internet website devoted to helping people hunt for jobs. Before long, I discovered the appeal of chatting—starting with people who tell you what a nice guy you are, how much they appreciate your wisdom and kind words, and provide positive reinforcement for being there in the first place. Unfortunately, I also got in over my head and went to the far extremes, taking my laptop everywhere, staying up late at night, logging on every weekend and getting caught up in a larger-than-life relationship with a very appealing woman. Anyone who thinks this can't happen to them needs to reconsider. I'm a well-educated man who was sure it could never happen to me. Well, here I am. I'm fortunate, in that my wife is one of those few individuals willing to stick by me and help me get over this nonsense. I'm going to try like hell not to let her down."

Fran is the wife of a surfer addict whose life has become a nightmare.

"My life, as I knew it, and my vision of the future have crumbled around me in the space of several months. My husband is addicted to chat. He minimizes his instant message screens whenever I walk into the room. He claims that women tell him their problems and these conversations are confidential, because these women trust him. But I'm his wife! He spends his energy meeting the emotional needs of others and he has no time for me. Our relationship is suffering while he spends hours just chatting with other women. I go to bed alone and I wake up alone. My husband has lied to me. He has hidden things from me. He barely tolerates me. He is rude and withdrawn. He has become a stranger to me. He claims this is all in my head. Occasionally I think of leaving him for a while. I cannot go on like this. My mental and physical health are deteriorating. I have tried talking to him, but he will not cooperate. I don't even think he will give me a second thought when I'm gone."

Joseph was in a very happy marriage for twelve years until his wife began using online chat rooms. Like Fran's husband, Joseph's wife was caught up in the ideal images that could be projected over the internet. Now, Joseph has been involved in a divorce and a very complicated custody battle because of it. His ex-wife began chatting as an occasional hobby. Eventually this "hobby" grew to be something that she could not do without. Once she found someone to talk to one-on-one her habit became even more demanding. It included extensive amounts of time spent online, phone calls, and the exchange of pictures and gifts. Joseph's children have also been coaxed into chatting with his ex-wife's newfound love. The time she spent online was in addition to the time she spent on the phone with this other man while at home and at her place of employment. Joseph and his ex-wife went to a marriage counselor for help, but the only thing that came out of these sessions was the counselor's advice that she was doing nothing wrong by spending several hours a day chatting with another man.

Joseph could not accept what the marriage counselor told him. He just could not believe that it was considered tolerable for his wife to spend significantly more time communicating with a fantasy than with her own husband and children. Now Joseph is trying to deal with the possibility of losing custody of his children to his ex-wife, who he fears will neglect them. He says, "I wish someone somewhere could do something about all the horror stories of all the families that have been destroyed by supposedly 'normal' people who insist on breaking their families apart to satisfy a selfish habit. There is never a winner in these cases, only losers—family, friends, children." Joseph believes it is too late to repair his ex-wife's situation since she filed for a divorce and is convinced she has fallen in love with her chat room friend, but I hope that it will not be too late for the other families who are in the middle of a similar situation.

Jessica met a young man on a chat program. The rest is troubled history.

"He was so much fun and we laughed constantly. Soon, I was rushing home to get online to talk to him, and we were sending each other emails to wake up and to go to sleep with. He lived in Europe and I was in California, so it was never a romantic interest. We were just close friends who could talk about anything. Then my daughter graduated from college and was sent on a four-week vacation to Paris as a present from her father. I went for the first two weeks and Andrew joined us there. Before the end of the first week, I knew that I loved him, and when he kissed me for the first time, I almost passed out. I saw black stars and was completely breathless. We walked around those quaint streets totally lost in our romance. Two weeks after returning home, I headed back to France to visit him for two weeks. We continued the relationship as it had been in Paris, except that now there were more serious issues to be considered. Several times I was going to leave, but just couldn't because I was so much in love with him. We continued our Internet romance once I returned to California. In October, I asked him to marry me. He said yes. We married later that year. That began the happiest two years of my life. Unfortunately Andrew could not find a job. As we entered our third year of marriage, Andrew became decidedly unhappy, and there was little I could do to help, as he completely shut me out. He began studying Italian like a fanatic and staying up all night online. Then I discovered that he was having an Internet affair with a person from Rome. She was four years younger than me, which he very rudely pointed out during one of our arguments. I could change my weight, color of hair and eyes, conversational language and learn computers. One thing I cannot change is my age. After two months of escalating horror, he finally left me, taking our dog Maxwell. It was the lowest point in my entire life. I felt as though my heart was completely ripped from my body.

"I thought I had found love, but now there is only the pain of forgetting and the heartache of being forgotten. Now Andrew wants nothing more to do with me, saying that it is best. For him, I am sure this is true. All I know is that it is unfair to show me what happiness is, then hurt me so badly by abandoning me.

"I sold my home, clearing out our debts with the proceeds, and moved to Switzerland, after being promised a job by a headhunter. When I arrived I was told that there was no job until I learned to read, write, speak, and understand German. So I went to school every day, studied every night, and walked my dog in between studying and school.

"There is not much fun in living right now, but maybe when I get a job and an apartment I can begin to live again. For now, I have refused to date because I have no interest in it.

"There are others out there like me. I pray that you can find a way to communicate to each other and not to the Internet. It seems, at first incredibly attractive, but it can destroy a great relationship."

Lydia is a forty-five-year-old woman who became very addicted to sex chat rooms. In the beginning, she says, she was just curious as to what people do and say in these chat rooms. Lydia explains that she is overweight and has low self-esteem. She was frustrated, because she still had sexual feelings, but felt that she had no one with whom she could share these feelings. She began to get involved in chatting with men in "sex rooms," where she could be whatever she wanted to be: young, attractive and exciting. Soon she met a man and came to enjoy chatting with him until early hours in the morning. She also received e-mails from this same man every morning and evening. They would write to each other and plan times to meet in the sex chat rooms. He sent Lydia e-mail greeting cards and she enjoyed the attention. After a few days of chatting, he gave her his phone number and she called him and talked about many things. They also engaged in phone sex for hours at Lydia's expense, because she would not give out her phone number. When she received her phone bill, she was afraid to open it right away and see how expensive it would be after their long conversations.

Lydia goes on to tell us how this online relationship almost cost her a close friend:

"I had gotten to the point where I was lying all the time to my good friend, because I knew that she wouldn't approve of what I was doing in these sex chat rooms. My friend caught me in many lies and I really felt bad about that, but I was also enjoying what I had with this man.

"I finally told my online friend the truth about me, or at least some of the truth and we ended this relationship of sex chats, phone sex and emails. I still think of him at times, but I know that it was wrong and I feel ashamed of what I had done.

"These chat rooms are addicting and if you are a weak person, it will cause you to lose loved ones that really matter and care about you for you. I found that out just in time…"

Nadia, like so many other people that have written and talked to me, has a codependency problem. She is also addicted to chat rooms. Nadia says that her relationship with her husband is suffering as a result of this. She is so addicted that she becomes very unhappy if her husband says that he will be home from work early. Yet before her addiction, it was fantastic when he got home early. Now she starts fights with him just so he will avoid her and allow her to go online and chat with her cyber friends. Nadia admits that she has even written to some of them giving her number and has arranged meetings with one particular "friend." Nadia explains how her addiction is affecting her priorities and her life:

"I would never have considered cheating on my husband before but now I feel like anything goes and I wouldn't care if my husband left as long as he left me the computer. Perhaps it is because when you are online you can be whoever you want to be and no one knows or cares. I guess the reason I am now seeking help is because of my rising phone bill. I am tired of having to lie to my husband to pay the bills and not let him see the phone bill when it comes in. I am no longer doing things I should for myself or the kids because I feel like I have to stop off at a cyber café or stay at home and surf as much as I can. Regardless of how stupid and meaningless it is, I feel I'm missing something if I don't go online."

Benny's wife, aged fifty-two, learned about chat rooms about four weeks before Benny and I spoke.

"About three weeks ago she began corresponding with a forty-five-year-old in another state. Since that time she has spent up to nineteen hours a day conversing with him. She now seems to be infatuated and they say that they love each other. Two nights ago she was on until 2:30 AM (6:30 his time), which means that he must have stayed up all night chatting with my wife, then gone to work. I believe he is a computer programmer. I caught the closing of one of his e-mails to my wife and I will paraphrase it: I miss you; I love you; I think of you all the time.

"Apparently his wife is not aware of what's going on, which makes me wonder what sort of aloof relationship they have. My wife and my relationship are cold and she says that she doesn't want to stop corresponding with this other man or get counseling. Our twenty-five-year marriage is on seriously rocky ground. Our three children and household are taking a back seat to 'him.' Yesterday, my wife didn't even change her clothes when she got home from work. Instead, she immediately went to a closed chat room."

Megan thought she met a wonderful man on the net and after some time, he asked her to marry him. She agreed and quit her job of fourteen years, although she has a child to support. The man, Gregory, said they would be married in February, when he came back from visiting his family in Brazil. Two weeks after his return, he refused to answer his phone when Megan called. He changed all of his online information, so Megan had no other way of getting in touch with him. Now she is hurt and suffering from very low self-esteem and regrets because her son was hurt as well.

Teenagers often don't tell the frightening truth about Internet hookups. But Felicia's is one story that parents should take seriously. While still in junior high school, she asked her parents to sign up for Internet service so that she could communicate with her friends online. At first they had doubts about the safety of allowing their daughter to surf the net, but eventually they agreed and became subscribers to a service. Two years after acquiring Internet access, Felicia noticed one day that she was unable to sign on with her Internet provider. When she contacted the service, she was told that her account had been terminated because it was being used to send pornographic materials to young children. Felicia and her parents argued that she had not been the sender of the inappropriate materials, since she was still very young and did not have access to a digital camera or scanner. Felicia herself was shocked when she was read the contents of one e-mail supposedly sent by her.

After speaking to Felicia's parents, the Internet provider agreed to reinstate their service, but similar events took place and eventually they decided to cancel their Internet service entirely in order to protect their daughter and themselves. As a high school student, Felicia occasionally uses the Internet for school projects and to chat with friends. She says that the service has improved somewhat, but she is still disturbed by some of the material she sees online.

Freddie tells another sad story of long-distance romance:
"I'm a mechanic on a freighter and it can be difficult to meet someone. I'm often in port for less then two days at a time and I've never been a very smooth talker so I thought I'd try an online dating site. I posted my profile and started shopping for the perfect mate. Almost two months later I met a woman online and started to get to know her... or so I thought. We emailed each other for a couple of weeks then decided to meet for coffee. She seemed very nice plus she

was easy on the eyes so I asked her out to dinner. She accepted my invitation and I set to work on reservations. I had to move fast because I was due back to work in about just a few days. The date went off without a hitch. In fact we had such a great time I ended up taking her home. We had sex all night and into the next day. For the rest of my break we spent almost all of our time together but the time came when I had to go back out to sea. Before I left I told her that I didn't expect her to commit to me because we simply hadn't known each other long enough but she insisted and said that I was what she was looking for. She came to visit me on the ship twice and both times we had great fun and the sex just got better and better. I really thought I had found my match. The first night after I came home was fantastic: we cooked dinner and we could hardly keep our hands off each other. During our conversation she let it slip that she had been seeing someone other than me but she assured me that I was the one she wanted. Suddenly things came into focus. Suddenly it was all clear to me... she slept with another man the night before I got to her house!!!! Even though I didn't expect a commitment from her she still made one to me and then she betrayed that commitment. I work on the ocean. I spend two months at a time at sea. The last thing I need is to have this hanging over me. It drives me crazy to think of her with another man, all the while telling me she loves me. I did the only logical thing I could think of—I left!"

Tania reveals that it is not only the young who fall for illusions on the internet. A forty-seven-year-old single divorced mother of a fifteen-year-old daughter, she felt that she had put her life on hold since divorcing her daughter's father ten years earlier. She hadn't dated in years and she felt it was time to get back into the social scene. She recently lost her job of seven years and just purchased a computer. She went to the cyber world to find people to talk with. That was where she met Eric. He was smart, witty and made Tania feel that they had many things in common. Their friendship developed quickly. Eric was six years her junior, but neither he nor she saw the age difference as a problem.

After a few weeks of communicating online, they exchanged addresses and telephone numbers. Eric spoke of love and possible marriage. Tania wasn't ready for marriage quite yet, but she was ready for a relationship. They made plans for her to visit him for a couple of days at his home. Tania had another online friend in the same area as Eric who was graduating from high school, so she planned to make it a double visit. However, when she told Eric of her plans, he became extremely angry, cursing, yelling and then hanging up on her. Later, he sent Tania an email saying how badly she had hurt him and wondering how she could be so "deceitful and mean." Tania relates the disappointing end of their relationship:

"After all the wonderful times Eric and I spent on the phone and online, it was suddenly over. I couldn't live the rest of my life with someone who was so possessive and could lose his temper so quickly and violently. I ended the relationship immediately and he began stalking me. Eric created an internet chat room just to discuss me with others online. He sat for hours watching my name on his buddy list and constantly checking my whereabouts online. I know this because he eventually admitted it. I became frightened, since I had given him my address. I reported him to his internet provider as a stalker, but all they did was advise me to block him from everything and ignore him and any contact he tried to make. This went on for months before he finally gave up and left me alone."

It is important to realize that not everyone one meets online is a weirdo. However, as I found out while researching this section of the book, it is even more important to recognize that there are no regulations overseeing relationships that begin on the net. Moreover, those who are needy and lonely are potential targets for male and female predators and scam artists of both sexes.

I received personal stories from people who surfed my website, where I asked that stories be emailed to me. Some people, though, wanted to speak with me personally and sent me instant messages. Mostly these were people who were making sure I wasn't into some scam. I explained the book in detail and asked that they send their stories to me. One instant message conversation I had shows in detail how the obsessive, odd and worse are able to seek out and prey on those opening themselves up for contact on the Internet.

I was working on my computer one night when I was contacted by an individual who said he had a story that I might be able to use in my book. I gave him my instant messaging screen name and he wrote to me. At first, our conversation seemed harmless enough: he told me a story about meeting a woman on the Internet, speaking to her on the phone and going on a date. Then he said that she had abruptly cut off all contact with him and never given him a reason. He asked me to send an email to this woman to ask her what had happened, even gave me her email address. When I told him I had to wrap up the conversation so I could get back to work, he continued to write to me, even after I repeatedly reminded him that I needed to go and tried to cut him off.

As you can see, this stalker approached me in just one meeting. Each time I ignored his message, he continued to write. When I said goodbye, he still continued. Every night for about a week, he tried to instant message me. When I tried to cut the connection off, he wanted to know why I was "dumping" him like the other woman did. Here was a person whose whole world was the Internet. He was looking for love, affection, attention, whatever, from complete strangers. I finally had to block his screen name to avoid further contact. The difference between reality and fantasy is a hard concept to grasp for some, and it's only magnified on the Internet.

Part
◄ 4 ►

You Are Not Alone—
Understanding, Acknowledging and Overcoming Copdependency

◀ 10 ▶

Strategies on Being Alone,
Not Lonely:
Being Comfortable Being You

One day my younger son had a soccer tournament. The freeway had a constant barrage of construction. Barrier walls on either side of the two lane highway closed in on us, giving the overwhelming feeling of claustrophobia and fear of being crushed. It was pouring down rain, as well.

In order to relieve a little of the pressure of driving and finding my way from place to place, darting in and out of traffic, merging where there was no room to merge, I elected to ride with the father of another player. Henry is a good-looking, intelligent man with whom it is easy to play the dumb blonde and sit back, allowing everything to be done for me.

While we were riding to lunch after the second game, he said to me, "Rebekah, I think that you really are smart. I think that you are an intelligent woman, and if you'd just get out of the rut you are in, you could be so much more." I tried to stutter out something to relieve my embarrassment at having been caught "playing dumb." He apologized and said he didn't mean anything untoward by his statement, but he was so right. All of my life I slacked off and waited for someone else to plot the course. Letting myself become a door-mat and then wondering why I've got tread marks all over me was a problem stemming from childhood. I have now learned that I have been abused, but only because I put myself in that position.

Few people I met in the course of my private life knew I have multiple master's degrees and even fewer know I have a stellar IQ. Yet to many of them I tell my stories of how I lost this, screwed up on that, did this wrong, etc. I, like many, feel the need to share every anecdote of my mistakes, hoping to make people laugh and hoping to make them like me. Somehow I felt that if I made someone feel good about themselves, i.e., made them feel smarter than me, maybe they would want to be around me more. As I learned to look deeper into myself I found that I made fun of myself first so that no one else had a chance to. I talked about my fat butt and my weight gain before anyone could make fun of me. I brought attention to all of my flaws so that others didn't have to. It was easier to clown and have people laugh at me on purpose than to be serious and have the same people laugh or worse yet, not pay attention to me at all. My life was about pleasing other people, instead of focusing on my own mental well being. Are you in that rut? Let's talk about how to get out.

It has been said that "comparison is the root of all inferiority." When looking at another person's strengths and comparing them to your own weaknesses, there is no way to come out feeling good about yourself. Self-image is often based on how we stack up against our peers. Not how tall or how smart we are, but who's the tallest? Who's the smartest? Who's the prettiest, the skinniest, the closest to perfect? Many adults leave a childhood of self-loathing and self-imposed ridicule and enter adulthood unprepared for the social challenges they are to meet. Self-worth shouldn't be based on the whims of birth or of social judgment, but on stressing the redeeming and positive qualities that you do have. The standards by which we measure our acceptability as human beings are arbitrary, temporary and unfair. The system undermines the confidence of young people and paralyzes its victims. Your personal worth should not be dependent on the opinions of others or the fluctuating values that those people represent. Every person is entitled to dignity, self-respect and confidence. Give yourself permission to enjoy these rights.

An important thing to remember is that parents should treat children with respect as well. Always be careful to take your child's thoughts and opinions seriously and be honest in your discussions with them. By doing so you can help them establish healthy self-esteem. Young children look up to their parents as their first role models and it is up to parents to set a good example and give children a solid foundation on which to build their characters. Here are some tips on the development of self-esteem in children:

▸ While young children look to their parents to gauge self-worth, older children will begin to rely on the opinions of the peers to shape self-esteem. Parents and teachers can be instrumental in helping children establish healthy relationships with peers.

▸ Children's evaluations of themselves may fluctuate according to how they think they are perceived by others, particularly friends and classmates.

▸ It is important to teach children core values in the family and reinforce them through examples.

▸ Children should be encouraged to come to parents with questions or problems. Communication is key, so there should be no "taboo" subjects.

▸ If a child is having difficulty with friends or classmates, he or she may have decreased self-confidence for a while. Let children know that they are valued and important to you, even if they have been made to feel otherwise by someone else.

▸ True appreciation of a child's qualities, achievements and interests is more effective in building self-esteem than empty, insincere or non-specific praise.

▸ Children respond well to challenges, as long as tasks are not too difficult to be completed with a reasonable amount of effort. Successfully completing a tricky task can give a great boost to a child's self-confidence.

▸ Delegating certain responsibilities or simple chores suited to a child's level of ability imparts a sense of belonging, importance and accomplishment.

▸ When children make mistakes or fail at something, it is important not to dwell on the failure, but to work on

finding ways to improve. The emphasis should be on learning from the experience and growing rather than on the
need to succeed at all times.

Cathy, a woman I respect a lot, told me recently that she understood why women stay in abusive relationships. Then she told me of
her own tremendous effort to get out of a relationship with a man
who beat her. I was shocked that a part of her wanted to stay with
him and expected the same kind of treatment in later relationships,
because today she is a very independent woman, but I felt drawn to
her story.

Cathy told me that she believes many women want to be sec-
ondary to their male partners. They want a man who will dominate
them. What such women really want is a man who is more intelligent, more masterful and more creative than the woman is. But since
that is rare, what they settle for instead is a man who will overpower
them. She said that it's a problem born of history, when the females
of most species were the subservient ones. And that being pro-
grammed from a young age to be gentle, sweet, receptive creatures,
they put up with abuse rather than assert themselves.

I have to admit that this idea makes more sense to me than the
idea that has been circulated most—that abused women lack self-
esteem. That is undoubtedly the case for many women, and being
abused further erodes self-esteem, but Cathy, who spent years in a
horribly abusive relationship, had no reason to have low self-esteem,
having been raised like a princess in a kind, loving, virtuous, upper-
class family.

The truly malignant effect of the notion that abused women are
weak and have low self-esteem is that it is doubly hard for such
women to leave their abusers. If women are constantly told that they
are weak, need protectors and cannot take care of themselves and
their children, this enforces their feelings of inferiority and incapac-
ity. The actual effect for most women is to encourage them to stay
with the people who hurt them longer, while they grow even more
reluctant to leave.

This image, I believe, has become popular due to collusion of media and societal pressures so that there are very few ways to break out of the downward spiral. Thus women stay with abusers, which would seem to indicate that women are doomed. But they aren't. Though the idea of women's desire to be subservient and men's desire to dominate has been perpetuated by past myths and cultures, this is only a part of the picture. The human mind and human will have a place in it as well. And these run by far different principles.

Educated women often find themselves on a battlefield between an ingrained desire to be subservient to men and their minds' desires to be equal to men. It is wrong to reduce men and women to their animal nature. Both women and men need to fulfill themselves, contributing to the world the talents they have to offer.

When someone has low self-esteem, willpower is not as strong and he or she is likely to doubt the worth of his or her own intellect. Therefore such people are likely to revert to the roles they have come to see as inevitable. Thus, low self-esteem men abuse women and low self-esteem women seek out abuse. Sometimes, as we have seen through the stories in thus book, these destructive roles are reversed, with women becoming the abusive agents. However, low self-esteem, as my friend Cathy's case shows, is not the sole reason for staying in abusive relationships.

Both women and men need equality in their personal relationships. Their needs may be very different in means but similar in end.

Roger gives a man's opinion on this subject:

"I'm a thirty-nine-year-old divorced male, considered good-looking, clean-cut, not in debt, responsible, etc. I'm organized, cook, clean, do laundry, do the finances, grocery shop, maintain the cars, do the yard work, am not into drugs or drinking, stay in constant contact with my daughters since the divorce, and basically am everything the average couch-potato is not, although I'm far from perfect…"

Since his divorce, Roger says, he has met women with all sorts of problems. Some were clingy, wanting to get too close too soon. Some have been in debt and Roger feels that they may have been looking for someone to "rescue" them. As a single father who actively cares for his children, Roger appreciates women who are involved with family, but he was bothered by the women he met who were completely wrapped up in their children's lives and happiness, trying to buy their children's affections rather than earn them.

According to Roger, self-confidence and good self-esteem are very important in making a woman attractive to a healthy, non-abusive man. He is equally adamant on the importance of compromise in relationships. As Roger reminds us, neither men nor women can be doormats or control freaks in a healthy, balanced relationship.

Each partner may come from a very different place in terms of past hurts and present desires, but each needs to develop self-esteem in order to foster a fulfilling, nurturing and non-codependent relationship. A few things that we can do for ourselves and our children to increase positive self concept are:

▶ Emphasize positive accomplishments.
▶ Do not compare oneself with others.
▶ Reject the idea that beauty, intelligence or athletic ability defines a person.
▶ Remember, whatever the conflict, this too shall pass.
▶ Until life ends, there is always a second chance; try, try again.

◀ 11 ▶

Child Abuse:
The Seeds of Self-Loathing
and Codependency

How do men and women become codependent? These may very well be roles thrust upon them from abused childhoods in which they learned the parts of dysfunctional relationships perhaps too well.

About five years ago, when I was going through my divorce, I realized I had to simplify my lifestyle to accommodate my dwindling financial state. I felt devastated to be taking my children from their middle class suburban home in a peaceful, safe neighborhood near their friends. Nevertheless, I couldn't afford to stay in that house or any house at that point. An apartment was our only option and memories sprang to my head of our apartment days when I was a teenager—kids playing in parking lots instead of green-grassed lawns, riding bikes between parked cars, playing baseball in the alley. I didn't want that for my kids, not at all. I didn't want my mistakes to take away what they deserved out of childhood. I searched wildly for the perfect place to live, somewhere cheap but livable, somewhere that the boys could play safely outside without fear of being hit by cars or shot by stray bullets. Most apartment complexes in our area have neither of those luxuries.

I was blessed to find an apartment building surrounded by fields on three sides and a bayou on the other side, with a view of million dollar homes less than half a mile away from our doorstep. There's a winding trail out back for them to ride their bikes or me to exercise—though to tell the truth, I've walked the trail fewer times than I'd like to admit. Directly behind our apartment is a field of grass for the boys to play ball or do whatever they like free from harm. It's a low crime area, deemed a "safe neighborhood with excellent schools." It was the perfect place; if I wasn't able to give them the best, this was as close as I could get. And so it went for the first year, no disturbances or anything to bring back my fears.

One afternoon, as I settled in after getting out of school, one of my son's friends came to the door saying that there were screams coming from the apartment above ours. There were four residences in our section and I knew the people in all but one, the one in question. In that one dwelled a single mother living with quite a few children. A constant string of people, mostly men, came in and out of her apartment and the children had been found, on occasion, wandering around outside and even knocking at our front door, even though we'd never met. A few times we were woken in the middle of the night to sounds of fighting and outside the window we'd see the woman arguing with various men and women. I was upset, but I said nothing to them or to the rental office. Neighbors spoke about it among ourselves—"What a shame, those poor kids, what a terrible way to raise them"—but we did and said nothing until that night.

I ran outside to the foot of the stairs and listened for a moment. I heard, through the thick wooden door, a little girl's screams and cries. Back around to the side of the building, directly under their window, the sounds were louder and I could hear a man's voice yelling as well, "Shut up, shut up!" The children I'd seen coming in and out of the apartment in the last few months were young, not even school-aged, and I could tell from the cries that it was one of the youngest ones. I ran up the stairs, banging my foot purposefully loud on each step. I was terrified. By the time I'd reached the door, the noises had stopped and it was eerily silent, standing right outside their home. I knocked on the door; beat on it, bruising my fist with the force I was using, but no one answered. Could I have been mistaken? Could it have been the television or another apartment? I felt it wasn't possible.

I sat on the bottom step for the longest time, waiting for the slightest sound. Then I called the police.

A short while later, I heard sirens outside my window. Finally the police were there. Even now, four years later, I'm shaking and in tears; it's vivid like it was yesterday. I raced outside, colliding with the EMS team looking for an apartment. I directed them upstairs. They didn't question my directions, just took the steps two at a time, nearly falling in their haste.

I stood at the foot of the stairs as three or four police cars rounded the corner and into the yard in front of my door. I pointed, and they followed in the footsteps of the others. The door slammed shut and I stood there forever, waiting for an eternity to find out that baby's future and if she would ever have one. Finally the door crashed open, the EMTs carrying the baby, skin and bones, on the stretcher. They ran at the speed of light to the ambulance and sped off, sirens blaring in the quiet afternoon. The little girl never came back.

The police took the man who was up there away in their car, leaving the other girls with me and a neighbor until family arrived to pick them up. I took the children, both under three, into my home. They were filthy. Not just playing in the mud, haven't taken a bath in a few days dirty. No, there was a horrid, putrid stench locked into their skin. Their hair was caked and natty, dirt and food stuck down to the scalp. They held onto me, not even knowing who I was, and wouldn't let go. I bathed them and found bruises shining on the skin, old ones and new. They winced as I rubbed the wash-cloth across their tender flesh, and I knew they were in pain. They didn't speak, didn't seem to know any words, or even the English language. After they'd been cleaned, I put them on the couch, bundled in thick, warm towels, and I went upstairs to find some clothes. What I found was dismal, wretched, nothing I could ever imagine. There was no furniture upstairs, no couches, beds, or chairs. There were no toys in the babies' room, no dressers, nothing. All of the clothes for the whole family were stuffed into a broken playpen in the center of one of the rooms and they were filthy, smelling of vomit and excrement.

I walked through the house, trying to imagine what had happened. In the bathroom, there was blood on the floor and the shower curtain was torn down. Eventually the prosecutor told me that there was blood found on the toilet base, and that was most likely where the final blow had taken place. I sat on the floor of that bathroom and cried like I'd never cried before. I found out later that the baby had been beaten so hard that her organs, her stomach, pancreas and bladder, had been punctured. She'd not been fed in a while, nor had the other children. The mother had taken off and left a boyfriend to watch the kids. No one could find her; it was as if she'd forgotten she had precious babies at home waiting for her. I thought of all the things that my kids had; video game systems, computers, their own television and all the accoutrements that go along with it. I make sure they get everything in my power to give them. And fifty feet away, children were dying of starvation and abuse. At least two of the girls had been sexually molested and some of the scars were months old.

I spent a year waiting to testify against the man who killed the little girl. He swore to the police that she'd fallen down the stairs, but with my testimony and the pattern of bruises and broken bones on her body, it was obvious what he'd done to her. Apparently the coroner could tell that this wasn't the first time she'd been beaten, and it wouldn't have been the last. I was able to help put him away in prison for the rest of his life, but that couldn't bring that baby back.

I still ask myself, what if I'd called when I first noticed things were strange in that apartment? What if I'd kept banging on that door instead of giving up so easily? My father's words were with me a lot through that time. She was in God's hands now. He'd called her to him because he knew her life wasn't right. I kept telling myself that, but I couldn't get over the guilt of standing by and doing nothing. I know I could have done more if I'd just stepped up, away from that fear, and stood up for those girls. I pray for them each day as I pray for my own children, and I hope that whoever's got them now is able to conquer their terrible beginning, the hideous memories of their youth.

The U.S. Department of Health and Human Services, Family and Children's Bureau gives us these startling statistics in their study, "Child Maltreatment 2002: Summary of Key Findings":[1]

▶ An estimated 896,000 children were determined to be victims of child abuse or neglect for 2002.

▶ More than 60 percent of child victims were neglected by their parents or other caregivers. Almost 20 percent were physically abused, 10 percent were sexually abused and 7 percent were emotionally maltreated. In addition, almost 20 percent were associated with "other" types of maltreatment based on specific state laws and policies.

▶ Children ages birth to three years had the highest rates of victimization at 16.0 per 1,000 children.

▶ Girls were slightly more likely to be victims than boys.

▶ American Indian or Alaska Native and African-American children had the highest rates of victimization when compared to their national population. While the rate of White victims of child abuse or neglect was 10.7 per 1,000 children of the same race, the rate for American Indian or Alaska Natives was 21.7 per 1,000 children and for African-Americans 20.2 per 1,000 children.

▶ More than one-half of all reports that alleged child abuse or neglect were made by such professionals as educators, law enforcement and legal personnel, social services personnel, medical personnel, mental health personnel, child day care providers and foster care providers. Educators made 16.1 percent of all reports, while law enforcement made 15.7 percent and social services personnel made 12.6 percent. Such nonprofessionals as friends, neighbors and relatives submitted approximately 43.6 percent of reports.

▶ Child fatalities are the most tragic consequence of maltreatment. For 2002, an estimated 1,400 children died due to child abuse or neglect.

▶ Three-quarters of children who were killed were younger than four years old, 12 percent were four to seven years old,

6 percent were eight to eleven years old and 6 percent were twelve to seventeen years old

▸ Infant boys (younger than one year old) had the highest rate of fatalities, nearly nineteen deaths per 100,000 boys of the same age in the national population. Infant girls had a rate of twelve deaths per 100,000 girls of the same age. The overall rate of child fatalities was two deaths per 100,000 children.

▸ One-third of child fatalities were attributed to neglect. Physical abuse and sexual abuse also were major contributors to fatalities.

▸ More than 80 percent of perpetrators were parents. Other relatives accounted for 7 percent and unmarried partners of parents accounted for 3 percent of perpetrators. The remaining perpetrators include persons with other (camp counselor, school employee, etc.) or unknown relationships to the child victims.

▸ Nearly 29 percent of all perpetrators of sexual abuse were other relatives and nearly one-quarter were in non-relative or non-child-caring roles.

▸ For calendar year 2002, an estimated 1,800,000 referrals alleging child abuse or neglect were accepted by state and local child protective services (CPS) agencies for investigation or assessment. The referrals included more than three million children. Of those, approximately 896,000 children were determined to be victims of child abuse or neglect by the CPS agencies.

▸ Approximately one in six boys is sexually abused before age sixteen.

▸ Abuse of multiple family members is common.[1]

Cindy tells a frightening story about her common law husband, saying that he has been very controlling of both her and her sons from a previous, abusive marriage. When they first began living together, they had an arrangement: Cindy would go to work and earn money to support the family, while Frank would stay at home and care for the house and her two sons. However, he has not honored his part of the agreement. Cindy tells me how she gets up every morning and finds herself doing the dishes she was too tired to wash the night before. On the weekends she cleans the house. Frank washes and dries the family's clothing on occasion, but he still expects Cindy or one of her sons to fold and put them away.

When the family is in need of groceries, Cindy and her sons go to the store to buy them. For over two years her oldest son was made to stay in his bedroom after school and on weekends because Frank had 'grounded' him, although it was unclear what he had done. Her sons were only allowed to eat meals with her on special occasions. They were not allowed to have friends come to the house or to go out after school. Both boys now have social problems at school, a fact that Cindy says is not surprising, since they are not allowed to interact normally with their classmates and peers. Cindy is not allowed to have friends either. Over the years, Frank has systematically denied her access to friends and loved ones from her past, so that she has gradually been cut off and left without a support system.

In addition to being extremely controlling, Cindy's husband is also verbally and physically abusive. She reveals that her oldest son has been pulled around by his hair and slammed into walls and that she has received similar treatment. Meanwhile her younger son has been forced to witness this violence. Frank controls every aspect of Cindy's life, even telling her how to dress and what type of makeup she should wear. Part of his manipulative behavior is to put Cindy on the defensive by accusing her of having affairs with other men. As she says, "If that were true, why would I have put up with his horrible treatment for so long?"

When Cindy became pregnant with her third child, Frank refused to believe that it was his for several months, despite the fact that she was so busy supporting him and her family that she had literally no free time away from home. After the baby was born, he expected Cindy to go on taking care of everything within days of her return from the hospital, even forcing her to go to the store by herself to buy groceries.

The youngest child is also subjected to Frank's controlling behavior, kept inside and confined to a playpen. Cindy fears that this will affect the baby's development. Her husband feels that he is doing all that is required of him just by staying home with the children and refuses to help with anything else.

Cindy attributes the source of Frank's anger and need to be in control to his experiences growing up in a sexually abusive family. According to his mother, he was abused by his stepfather for years, although he refuses to speak about it. Cindy wants him to get help, but knows that there is nothing she can do until he seeks out the help he needs himself.

Cindy has let Frank know that she no longer wants to be with him. Frank's family has said that they are willing to help her leave him out of concern for the children. He promised to change, to work on improving their relationship, but when Cindy suggested that he get professional help, he refused. Despite his promises, he is still verbally abusive and very little has changed. Cindy, although codependent, is working to break the cycle of abuse carried on by Frank:

"I have taken steps to leave the situation. The only difficulty now is to figure out how. I am lining up day care for my children and legal aid for myself. I'm ready to start over; I hope there's not been too much damage to my children already. I wish I hadn't stayed this long."

We've touched in other chapters on the long-term, harmful effects of child abuse in its many forms. Just as drinking, smoking and drug use in the formative gestational months have a detrimental physical and mental effect on children, abuse during the early years of youth causes life-long pain from the trauma. Self-esteem is lost and never found, or never established to begin with. Children grow up believing they are not worthy of real, healthy love. They feel less than adequate, not quite human, and, as adults, find partners and friends who are similarly abusive. So many children are physically abused each year by someone close to them, and thousands of children die from their injuries. For those who survive, the emotional scars are deeper than the physical scars.

These emotional scars can be caused by any of several different types of child abuse. The web site helpguide.org gives a comprehensive breakdown of child abuse and the many forms it may take.

Child abuse can be defined as any action that is potentially damaging to a child's physical or emotional health and development. Neglect is also a form of child abuse, in which a caretaker's failure to act or properly attend to a child's basic needs can result in physical or psychological harm. Child abuse may occur when a caretaker fails to nurture the child, physically injures the child or relates sexually to the child.

There are four major types of child abuse: physical abuse, sexual abuse, emotional abuse and neglect. Exploitation, or the use of a child for the benefit of caregivers or others, is another distinct type of abuse. An example of exploitation is child labor, which uses children for commercial reasons and can be detrimental to their development in various ways.

The first major type of child abuse, physical abuse, is defined as any non-accidental physical injury to a child inflicted by a parent or caretaker. Even when a resulting injury in unintentional, if the action that caused the injury was intentional, it is considered abuse. Some examples of abusive behavior are

> Beating with the hands or an object
> Whipping
> Punching
> Slapping
> Pushing or shoving
> Shaking
> Kicking
> Throwing
> Pinching
> Biting
> Choking
> Smothering
> Hair-pulling
> Burning with any hot object
> Any severe physical punishment inappropriate to a child's age

Physical abuse is different from corporal punishment, which is meant to inflict physical pain but not result in actual physical injury. Furthermore, corporal punishment is carried out with the specific purpose of disciplining a child, while physical abuse is carried out without a distinct purpose, but as a result of an adult's aggression. While corporal punishment is by definition different from physical abuse, it can escalate to the point that it becomes abusive.

The second major type of child abuse, sexual abuse, consists of any sexual act between an adult and a child. This includes a wide range of behaviors. Some examples are

- ▸ Touching or kissing a child's genitals
- ▸ Making the child touch the adult's genitals
- ▸ Any type of penetration, intercourse, oral sex or sodomy
- ▸ Exposing the child to adult sexuality in other forms (showing sex organs to a child, forced observation of sexual acts, showing pornographic material, telling "dirty" stories, group sex including a child)
- ▸ Violations of privacy

Acts of this nature are considered child abuse when they are committed by someone who is responsible for the child in some way, such as a caretaker, parent or other relative. Sexual acts committed on children by strangers are considered sexual assault. Laws regarding sexual abuse differ throughout the United States and the world due to widely differing ideas of what is appropriate and at what age a person is considered an adult rather than a child.

Sexual abuse can be particularly emotionally damaging to a child because he or she is likely to feel powerless compared to an adult abuser and may be trained to obey adults in authority despite the feeling that something is wrong. Complications arise through the adult's need for secrecy and the negotiations that must take place to maintain the child's compliance. While children's behavior and reactions may differ significantly and even seem seductive or inappropriate, this is because they have no mature means of understanding what is happening to them. Sexual abuse is never the fault of the child, as it is the responsibility of the adult to establish and maintain proper boundaries.

The third major type of abuse is emotional abuse. This is defined as any attitude, behavior or neglect by a caregiver that is damaging to a child's mental health or social development. Emotional abuse may include verbal abuse, such as habitual name-calling or insults, ignoring or rejection, withholding affection, threats or deliberate attempts to frighten a child, extreme forms of punishment such as prolonged solitary confinement, and excessive yelling or screaming at a child.

Emotional abuse is somewhat unique in that it can be carried out not only by a caregiver or responsible adult, but also by other children, such as siblings or unfriendly classmates. Emotional abuse frequently corresponds with other types of abuse and is closely related to some aspects of neglect, the fourth major type of child abuse.

Neglect is a failure to provide for the child's basic needs and may be carried out on a physical, educational or emotional level. Physical neglect may include inadequate provision for a child's basic needs, abandonment or lack of age-appropriate supervision. Educational neglect occurs when an adult fails to enroll a child of mandatory school age in school or to provide necessary special education. Excessive absences from school with a parent's knowledge or consent may also qualify as educational neglect. Emotional neglect is a lack of emotional support and love. This may include a lack of affection or expression of affection, exposing a child to domestic or other forms of violence, or exposing a child to drug or alcohol use.

A number of factors may influence what is considered emotional neglect. Different families may have different cultural values or traditions, varying standards for child rearing or different levels of income which affect a parent or caretaker's abilities to give children proper care and attention.

Child abuse can have a number of grim consequences, especially as abused children mature into adults. They may become emotionally unavailable to others or alienated from family members, suffer from low self-esteem, depression, addictions or mental illness, or become abusive themselves.[2]

Liz, like many others who have moved from abuse to codependency, has a complex story that spans many years. It is only in the past several years that, with the help of her husband and an exboyfriend, she was able to make connections between various events in her life to discover the truth. These two men clearly perceived things that Liz herself could not. Now she has come to realize that not only did her father abuse her at a very young age, but her mother and father selfishly used her for their own gain.

Liz has been raped several times, once at knife point by four men who threatened to kill her. She has also survived two terribly abusive relationships, one in which she was brutally beaten several times, the other a sixteen-year ordeal that destroyed her sense of self-worth through mental, physical and emotional abuse. Still, nothing compares to the feelings she has when she remembers what her parents did to her.

"I still don't know how to talk about it. My heart is pounding, my hands are shaking and I've gotten a headache. I almost don't know how to start.

"I don't have any recollection of my father abusing me when I was young, but when my husband suggested it, my gut said it was true. Apparently after an incident when I was very young (which my mother has never talked about), my father was never allowed to give us baths (not even the boys), or be near us when we changed. My mother kept him away from us during any physically sensitive time. She didn't even like him to rub my back (which I loved!). I can't imagine what he did, but I know he did something. Later, when I was older and my father had had a bit to drink, he would sometimes say things and touch me in ways that made me feel very uncomfortable. I never told anyone. What he may have done to me is too devastating for me to think about. I pretended these things never happened. He was my FATHER. What could I do? In those days you didn't talk about sexual child abuse—didn't talk about child abuse at all. If anyone had talked about these things, they would have realized that we were most certainly abused. But I would not have applied it to myself. I idolized my father. How could he do anything bad to me?"

At the age of fourteen Liz was forced to sleep with her father's boss. She recalls waking up at night to find a fat man, naked, sliding under the sheets of her bed. He told her that if she told anyone, her father would be fired. As long as Liz continued to have sex with

Harold, her parents got a lot of extra perks. They freely took advantage of this opportunity. Meanwhile, she hated him. To this day she has a severe aversion to overweight men.

When Liz was fourteen her family lived in Greece on the first floor of an apartment building. Her parents lived on one side of the hall and their five children lived on the other. Liz says that she never even thought of how Harold got into the apartment at night, since he needed a key. While Harold was there she tried to be quiet because she didn't want to wake her younger siblings.

Liz describes a skiing trip her family took with Harold. He bought her numerous gifts in an attempt to win her over. At one point they were in the car with Liz's parents and she was made to sit in the backseat with Harold, who constantly caressed her and commented on her soft, smooth skin. She wondered why her parents didn't seem to hear his remarks.

When she was fifteen Liz was sent to a boarding school in France. She hated it there, but even worse was the fact that Harold had permission to take her out for weekends and holidays. He wanted to buy her gifts, but she was afraid that someone would ask about the expensive presents. His solution was to give her small, expensive gifts, which Liz had to say that she had found if she was questioned. She remembers her mother smiling when she struggled to explain how she had found a ring in the airport. Harold had also given her a number of other tiny gifts, which were very expensive. Liz says of this situation, "It was so hard to explain. Now I know the reason my mother was laughing the way she was when I tried to explain where and how I had gotten these things—she KNEW where everything had come from. I had to go with Harold or he would fire my dad."

Liz finally put a stop to the abuse when she was sixteen. She said she didn't care what happened, and her father lost his job soon afterwards. Her parents were very cold and vindictive to her for a time, but she didn't immediately realize the connection between her rejection of Harold, her father's unemployment and her parents' treatment of her. She felt that if she told her mother, the answer she would have gotten was, "you must've done something to deserve it." Liz also doubts whether or not her mother would have believed her about the abusive relationship with Harold. She felt despair that she believes she will never forget.

Liz's father died a few years before she spoke to me, but she reveals that she never confronted him. She has never openly confronted her mother either, feeling that she would deny that there had been any abuse and Liz's accusations would only cause hard feelings. But she still struggles with the questions of how her parents could have used her in this way, submitting her to such awful experiences for their own personal gain.

I never knew abuse like this existed before I started teaching in a low-income area, but now I see it so much it's almost become routine. If not for my experience with the death of my neighbor, it might have become routine, but I won't let it. I watch every child with an eagle eye, like they were my own. And not all forms of abuse reveal themselves as bruises or broken bones. Neglect is a silent form of abuse, detrimental in its own way. I have students for whom neglect is a way of life.

One year I had a young man in my class, seven years old to every one else's six due to failing kindergarten early on. He was afraid to speak, afraid to make eye contact with anyone, especially adults. Every day he showed up at school anywhere from fifteen minutes to two hours late, missing reading, the subject he needed most. But for most of these children, survival and the basic necessities are their only concern.

When I finally got him to speak to me about his home life, he said that most times his mom never came home, and when she did, she was drunk or high. For a seven-year-old to even know these words was abhorrent to me. He said that he woke up by himself every morning, got up and came to school. He never ate breakfast and got here too late for the school breakfast. This didn't matter, because his mom wouldn't be bothered to fill out the free lunch form, so he wouldn't have been able to eat anyway. The office and I sponsored his lunch most days until we finally sent home enough lunch forms that his mom got tired of seeing them and sent one back. My sons and I won a small television and we gave it to him because he had no television at home, but most days he had no electricity at home. His mother was unreachable because the phone line was disconnected and he was unable to bathe or wash his uniforms because the water bill hadn't been paid. I washed his uniforms for him and sent him to the bathroom in the mornings to clean himself up. He told me his daddy and his momma's other boyfriend were both in jail, and that his momma had been there a bunch of times. Though this boy wasn't physically abused, his emotional scars will last a lifetime. What is the saddest to me is that he doesn't even know that there's a better life out there. As broke as I am, as much as my kids and I have to struggle from paycheck to paycheck, they are never without anything that they need. And I love them, I tell them every day, more than they want to hear. I hold them and hug them, though that's getting harder the older they get.

Sadly, this is not an isolated case in my classes or others. In more than half the schools in my city, in cities all across the state, in all fifty states, children are physically or sexually abused, or neglected. My students go home, at six years old, to no parent, no adult, no one. They are left to fend for themselves for nourishment in a home with no running water or electricity. Often they wear the same clothes for weeks on end, with no bath or substantial meals in all that time. I am scared to see these children in ten years; I'm terrified of will happen to them in the future. Each and every one of them has so much potential, but everything I do at school is lost when they get home. No one reads to them or studies with them or cares what grades they get. Though I've met exceptional and wonderful parents since I've been teaching, they are few and far between. I want to take each of these children home and show them what life should really be like. But poverty alone is not an indicator of abuse.

Annette is a twenty-two-year-old woman who was physically and emotionally abused by her stepfather for thirteen years. She describes him as a horrible, evil man. One of the things she remembers most vividly is that every time she was bruised or bleeding because of something her stepfather did to her, he laughed. If she cried because of something he said to her, he found it funny. According to Annette, "Inflicting that kind of suffering on a child is one thing. Laughing at it is EVIL."

Despite this, Annette told me that she can remember a few good times, a few nice things about her stepfather, but they were the exceptions that proved the rule. She remembers being taken out to help pick out the family Christmas tree because she had "the best eye for it" and she remembers her stepfather standing up to her mother over what Annette was allowed to wear to an awards ceremony at her school.

More than that, though, Annette remembers a lot of pain that she now knows she did not deserve. She remembers being punched in the stomach for forgetting to take out the trash. She remembers a lot of black eyes and mumbled excuses that teachers and friends accepted but did not really believe. She remembers telling everyone that she broke her wrist falling out of a tree. And the abuse she suffered wasn't just physical—Annette also remembers being called stupid, useless, worthless, fat, ugly, dumb, someone who would never amount to anything, a waste of space. Meanwhile, her mother stood aside and allowed the abuse to take place. She never stood up for her daughter and even told Annette it was her own fault on the rare occasions when her daughter appealed to her for help.

After years of this treatment, Annette started to feel stupid and useless and worthless. She stopped caring, stopped trying to get on her stepfather's good side, which angered him and led to more abuse. At the age of fifteen, she finally fought back and was thrown out of the house by her mother and stepfather. She was taken in by her grandparents, who were able to provide a more stable and supportive environment. Annette remembers her mother dropping her off with one suitcase and her guitar for "a little while." After her mother left, her grandparents told her that she was staying forever.

Six months after leaving her stepfather's house, Annette tried to commit suicide. She remembers thinking that the damage done to her was so painful and so deep that she would never get over it and be able to live a normal life. In the hospital as she was recovering, Annette's mother insisted that she see her stepfather. "Don't you want to see your daddy?" Although the abuse she had suffered at her stepfather's hands was the cause of her suicide attempt, Annette did eventually agree to see him. He told her again that she was stupid and he hoped she would be locked up for "a good long time so I could see how stupid I was."

Eventually Annette was able to get the help that she really needed. After she was released from the hospital, her stepfather was investigated for child abuse for the first and only time. He told the social worker it was his stepdaughter's fault—and unbelievably, his excuses were accepted. Annette says, "I'll never forget that. Ten years of abuse, and she let him brush it off with three words. Everything I'd accomplished, all the work and therapy went right out the window under a flood of hatred and rage. I hated him for blaming me for what he did. I hated the world for believing it was my fault. And deep down I hated myself for believing I might get some justice.

"He died in a car accident last spring. He drove his truck off a bridge while he was drinking. When my mom called to tell me, I couldn't even lie and tell her I was sorry. It's been months and I still haven't shed a single tear for him—I just don't feel any grief or remorse. It's not denial; I just don't feel it.

"I went to his grave, though, the last time I visited home. I guess I felt I had to say some kind of goodbye. But all I could think of, as best I can remember it, was 'Fuck you, Daddy. I'm glad you're gone, I hope you suffered, and I hope you're roasting in that Catholic hell you believed in.' I guess I feel like I finally got justice. Does that make me a horrible person? Maybe. But I won't deny or lie about how I felt, except to my mother. I've never said anything about my feelings to her, but I think she knows.

"There is one thing that I'm proud of—I broke that cycle. I have a four-year-old daughter, and I make a conscious effort every single day not to hit her or put her down, and to always, always give her the support and love and encouragement that I never had. She's a wonderful girl, and she is my whole life. And to tell the truth, I'm glad she'll never have to know my stepfather as a grandparent. That's one influence she's much better off without.

"You can make it. It isn't easy, and a lot of the time it's an uphill fight that you won't think you'll ever win, but you can make it. Just don't ever, ever stop fighting back."

According to an article entitled "Long-Term Effects of Child Sexual Abuse," by Peter E. Mullen and Jillian Fleming, "Being sexually abused is one of many painful and potentially damaging experiences that a human being may suffer in childhood. Whether and to what extent child abuse and neglect have negative effects depends on a variety of factors—related to the abuse itself, but also to relationships, in which the abuse and the child's responses occur." The article goes on to describe the various negative effects that sexual abuse can have on an individual's self-esteem. Interestingly, while lowered self-esteem is a common characteristic of survivors of sexual abuse, it is not the individual's opinion of his or her intrinsic worth that is most affected, but rather the individual's outlook on events in the outside world. Adult survivors of sexual abuse are more likely to anticipate unpleasant events in their lives and less likely to feel that they are able to influence events around them, contributing to a sense of hopelessness and futility.[3]

The most current statistics from the U.S. Department of Health and Human Services indicate that there are a number of factors that can influence the lasting effects of child abuse, particularly sexual abuse. Among these factors are the age of the child when the abuse occurred, the relationship of the child to the abuser, whether anyone else knew about the abuse and how he or she reacted to it, the degree of violence involved in the abuse, and the duration and frequency of the abuse. Other factors that may have some bearing on the lasting effects of child abuse are whether the abuse was designed to deliberately humiliate the child, how the type of abuse was viewed by family members or in the community and what type of support system and relationships the child has apart from the abuser.[4]

Children are most likely to be abused in a single-parent home and the most common physical abusers of young children are mothers, rather than fathers, stepfathers or boyfriends. A study by the Department of Health and Human Services shows that women comprised almost two-thirds of all child abusers and mothers accounted for 55 percent of child murders according to a Justice Department report.[5] According to Maggie Gallagher, the author of *The Abolition of Marriage*, "The person most likely to abuse a child physically is a single mother. The person most likely to abuse a child sexually is the mother's boyfriend or second husband."[6]

Danny tells us of his experiences with child sexual abuse beginning at the age of seven and the negative consequences this held for him as an adult. Danny's parents divorced while he was still very young. By the time he was six years old, his mother had gotten remarried to a man whose favorite hobby was making home movies. He was also an alcoholic who began physically abusing Danny not long after the marriage.

Danny's stepfather belonged to a small club that met periodically and filmed the children of various group members. This seemed like a normal activity to Danny at the time. Then when he was seven his stepfather took him to a club meeting without his mother. At this meeting, he told Danny to do things that he thought were strange, such as taking off his clothes and playing with other children. As a young child, Danny did not know what to make of this, but felt that he could not protest because his stepfather was an adult and in charge. Afterwards, he was told not to tell anyone what had happened at the club. Danny's stepfather threatened to injure Danny and his younger sister of he ever told. He remained silent in order to protect his sister.

As Danny got older the "games" at the club got worse. He was made to "play" with adults while others in the group filmed. Occasionally Danny's stepfather took his sister to meetings as well and told Danny to abuse his sister. He refused, but suffered beatings and other violent punishment for his lack of cooperation. As an adult, Danny still feels that he should have done more to protect his sister from the abuse that they both suffered. He was able to escape his stepfather when he was twelve and went to live with his biological father, but he is still haunted by memories of what his stepfather did to him as a child.

Research has shown that child abuse has a variety of lasting, negative effects, including drug and alcohol abuse or addiction, the development of eating disorders and an increased risk of suicidal tendencies.[7] Child abuse also seems to increase the risk of developing medical problems that eventually lead to hospitalization.[8] Child abuse has also, as we have seen, been linked to poor self-esteem, depression and an increased incidence of psychiatric problems.[7] Individuals who were abused as children are more likely to make poor choices of partners as adults, often entering into relationships that prove to be abusive.[9]

Yolanda is a survivor of extreme and consistent abuse as a child. When Yolanda was six months old an aunt found bruises covering most of the infant's body. Yolanda is uncertain who was responsible for these signs of abuse but believes that both of her parents were somehow involved. As a result of the vicious abuse she suffered from a very young age, Yolanda developed a dissociative disorder.

When she was three years old, Yolanda's father began sexually abusing her. She claims that she witnessed her father severely injuring another child and that he threatened her with various weapons, causing her to live in a constant state of fear. The experience was made worse by Yolanda's feeling that her mother at least suspected that the abuse was taking place but did nothing to stop it. She grew up feeling unwanted and unloved by either of her parents. Her need for approval was so great as a result of this that she worshipped her father, despite his continuing abusive treatment. Her disorder also helped her in denying that she had been so grossly mistreated.

Yolanda relates that she had no conscious knowledge that she had been abused as a child until she had her first flashback as an adult. She was not in therapy at the time and had never even considered that she might have been abused by her father. The flashback occurred during an argument with her husband, causing her to revert to very childish behavior and startling her husband, who felt he had "inadvertently hit upon a very sore spot" in Yolanda's past. Soon after that the flashbacks became more frequent and vivid, until she began to question her own sanity. The fear associated with these hidden memories was particularly unnerving for Yolanda.

The year that she began having flashbacks, Yolanda was hospitalized seven times. During her third hospitalization she was diagnosed with multiple personality disorder. She is believed to have over 150 full-fledged alters and fragment personalities. According to Yolanda, as a result of the abuse she suffered as a child and her subsequent development of this condition, "I am disabled. I cannot recall what my children's names are some days. I cannot see a man in a position of authority without feeling intense fear. I cannot handle money well and yet I have children to care for..."

Victims have to live with the trauma of what has happened to them for the rest of their lives, while the abusers appear to be able to put the past behind them as if nothing ever happened. Saying sorry does not change anything: a victim is still a victim. Sometimes an apology can change things for all people involved and victims do not have to remain victims; they can move on to become survivors. Offender recovery is much easier than survivor recovery, but both are not only possible but desirable.

The cycle of abuse can be broken by being careful to provide children with the care, attention and affection that they need, especially in the early years of life. Children who grow up in supportive, healthy environments are very unlikely to become abusers or to remain in abusive relationships as adults. The more developmental advantages a child has, the more likely he or she is to acquire a positive outlook on life and to make healthy choices later on. This is why it is so important to treat children with affection, courtesy and respect, in addition to taking care of their physical needs. By treating children as competent, capable and worthwhile individuals, parents and other adults can help build good self-esteem. And good self-esteem is very important in discontinuing the cycle of abuse that can stretch over generations.[10] Help protect your child from becoming either a controller or a doormat in a codependent situation.

◄ 12 ►

Success Stories:
Surviving Hell and Becoming
Independent

Remember, every step you take is a step away from where you used to be. No matter how deep the hole you're stuck in, I believe God's strength and love is always deeper. Some days you may think you'll never get through this mess, this relationship, this breakup, this life. But I have learned it's your choice which path to take. It's all up to you, how and when you get where you are going. It's all up to you where your game piece lands and what you make of your property when you get there. It's not up to your husband or wife, your ex boyfriend or girlfriend, your mother, your plumber. It's all up to you.

It's amazing, when I sit down to think about it, how I've come to be on the path I'm on now. Today I'm happy with where I am and where I'm going. Ten, twenty years ago, I never would have thought I'd be teaching, but I love it! I can't imagine doing anything else. I never would have gotten off track from my original plans if I hadn't abruptly become a single mother. And I surely never would have taken the time to write a book if I wasn't a teacher. So I truly believe that what I'm doing now is what was meant to be. All things happen for a reason. I'm right on track—after some slight derailments, of course.

Sure we're somewhat broke (we've driven home from Memphis hoping to make it on one tank of gas so we wouldn't be counting out dirty pennies from under the truck seats). But my boys and I are very close and I'm home every day when they get home. I don't work all hours like I would have in the medical field. I'm home on vacations and holidays and all summer to make sure they're growing up to be strong, sensitive men.

Anyway, my point is, after all my struggling and kvetching and falling deeper and deeper, I'm building a new life. You can too. My days of degradation are few and far between and I use the twelve-step plan I will be giving you to work through them. I've surrounded myself with a network of people who love me for who I am and what my strengths are. And that, my friends, is a monumental step for me. I know, as you will too, that each step, no matter how big or small, takes me further from where I used to be and toward the independent self I want to be and building a fulfilling relationship.

Through my research I have met and come to know others who've walked the path to strength. Among them is Harriet, who says, "The first man I ever loved was an alcoholic. He was a handsome, fun-loving man. He was my father. Played until the streetlights came on with the kids in the neighborhood, spent summers at the community pool and walked to the local grade school. As I got older I began to see that my friends had more than me. My brother and I shared a used bike, I only had one Barbie, and my clothes came from the Goodwill. I know now where the money was going."

Harriet goes on to describe how her father's alcoholism affected her as she matured. As a teenager she had very low self-esteem and felt inferior to everyone around her. Her parents contributed to her feelings of worthlessness, frequently telling her that she needed to lose weight or that she would never amount to anything. Some of Harriet's classmates picked up on her low self-esteem and singled her out as an easy target for teasing at school. It wasn't until she was in high school that Harriet found a group willing to accept her. Unfortunately, this group became involved with alcohol and drugs. In an effort to fit in, Harriet began drinking and using drugs as well. She says that she went to school high or drunk more and more frequently, feeling that people liked her better when she was high. Her drug use also helped her to forget the negative feelings she had about herself.

When Harriet was fifteen her parents divorced, remarried and had two more children each, leaving her feeling unwanted and out of place. To escape her loneliness, Harriet spent more and more time partying with friends, eventually moving in with and marrying a man who was an alcoholic. They had a son together, but the marriage did not last. Soon Harriet and her son were on their own, until she met and married a new man, also an alcoholic. According to Harriet, "I didn't see the pattern until it was almost too late. But it's never too late."

Harriet was disturbed to see that as her son grew, he seemed to be following the same path that she had traveled as a young woman. He had difficulty at school and at home with his stepfather. He began to drink and get into trouble, which made their home life increasingly tense. Harriet's husband fought with her son, while she attempted to smooth things over and keep them apart. The stress of trying to maintain peace in her family caused Harriet to have health problems and soon led to clinical depression.

When Harriet's son was eighteen, she decided to go to group therapy. She remembers going to the first session crying, convinced that she was a horrible person. She was genuinely surprised when other members of the group assured her that she was not. They also told her that she was not responsible for the problems between her husband and son or for her son's problems outside of the home. As Harriet says, "I had a lot of 'buts' and they had an answer for every one of them."

That first group therapy meeting was the beginning of a long recovery process for Harriet. She began going to three or four meetings a week and to local meetings of Al Anon. She says it took a long time before she was able to apply tough love and tell her son he had to move, but today she feels that she did it in God's time, not her own. She saw a counselor every week, sometimes several times a week. Gradually she created a new circle of friends, ones who did not judge or advise, but listened and helped when she asked them to. Harriet was finally able to find the inner strength that she never knew she had, the independence that others had smothered in attempts to control her.

In the years since she began seeking help, Harriet has made amazing progress. She says of her recovery, "I learned that codependency was a weight, a cancer, eating away at my very core, and not stopping there, but poisoning my whole world. What a weight lifted when I realized that! I learned to separate what was mine and what was not. I have serenity today that I never could have dreamed of. Now I sleep all night. Today I love who I am.

"I continue to grow daily. I am one year into my medical residency at middle age; I am almost a real doctor. I am still amazed and so pleased with myself. I'm so proud of me, and the people that matter have stuck with me through it all. I can't wait for the rest of my life!"

Nan tells another story of growth. Growing up, she witnessed a codependent mother and a father who was addicted to alcohol. Her father frequently berated her and belittled her mother, making them take turns feeling awful. Nan's mother said nothing in her own defense, so Nan learned to say nothing as well. She also learned to blame her problems on her situation at home. She told herself that nothing that went wrong in her life was her own fault, but at the same time she suffered from very low self-esteem. She says of herself, "the only time I felt like I was SOMEBODY was when I was drinking or letting boys have their way with me."

One day Nan realized that alcohol was becoming very important to her, to the extent that she started drinking at home by herself every day until she either passed out or blacked out. She also drank in bars, frequently waking up the next day unable to remember how she had gotten home. She drank in order to forget her problems, the mistakes she felt she had made and how unhappy she was with her life. She also drank to cover up her feelings of inferiority and failure. When she first made the decision to stop drinking she was miserable, struggling to overcome her addiction and deal with the negative feelings she had been ignoring for so long. Finally, after seven months, Nan agreed to go to a meeting of Alcoholics Anonymous. According to Nan, "That is the day my life started changing. I wanted what I saw in those rooms—especially the LAUGHTER! But I had no idea how to get it and I spent the first three years in AA questioning whether I was or was not alcoholic. Whether or not I was codependent. Whether or not I was trying to please everyone but me, controlling everyone while being controlled. Could I really be all of those?

"I was all of those things. As soon as I believed in myself, something strange happened. Everyone else began to believe in me too. Or maybe they always did, and I just couldn't see it. I cleaned up my credit, cleaned up (and cleared out) my love life. I made a promise to myself to be single for a year and sober for a lifetime. When I decided that I was a strong, able minded woman, and that a man was not necessary to survive, all of a sudden there seemed to be so many choices. Not the alcoholic abusers, verbally scathing, physically demanding, that always seemed to line up on my doorstep, but normal guys. And I let them know up front that I was making a change, and let them know what kind of man I was interested in. I let them know that under no uncertain terms would I waver from what was right for me."

Once she discovered her own self-worth, Nan found there was no limit to what she could accomplish. She took out a small loan and began her own flower shop, which has spread over five cities. She is currently engaged to a man who loves her exactly as she is, for who she is, and is extremely happy with her life. She knows that she will never achieve perfection, but she no longer expects to. As Nan says, "I'm just thrilled at living my life fully and no longer being controlled by others. Although it's been and still is and will always be a struggle against codependency, I know I can make it. I've come so far and have so much farther to go."

Strength grows slowly and in different ways, as Lynnette's story shows. She was adopted as an infant and can remember telling this to her kindergarten class during show-and-tell. She recalls this as the point at which she began to feel that she did not fit in with others.

Lynnette describes her adoptive parents as being "somewhat odd." They rarely spoke to their daughter directly or complimented her achievements or successes. However, they were often critical and did not hesitate to point out Lynnette's shortcomings. She was a very nervous from an early age and developed some peculiar tendencies. She also became very codependent, desperate to make her parents like her. As she says, "I would bend over backwards for them to no avail."

By the time Lynette entered the sixth grade, her unusual behaviors and codependency had become apparent. The smallest change in plans or routine was greatly disturbing to her. She recalls an experience at a summer camp when she was so upset by the change of environment that she made herself sick. She cried almost the entire time she was there and barely ate anything. She was unable to spend even one night away from home without serious problems and she was afraid and embarrassed by her behaviors.

When she entered junior high school, Lynnette's difficulties were compounded by the feeling that she was somehow not as good as her peers, that she was not quite "right." While these are common emotions for children at this age, Lynnette's reaction was extreme. She began injuring and mutilating herself to avoid group activities that made her uncomfortable. Eventually she became addicted to the act of injuring herself. She also made herself into a doormat for her friends and classmates, doing favors for them in order to get attention and approval. She would do anything the other girls at school told her to. Without any positive reinforcement at home, she struggled to get some at school.

When Lynnette started dating, she quickly became almost obsessed with her first boyfriend. Once again, in an attempt to gain approval and acceptance, she submitted to whatever he asked of her. She says that she would have done anything for him, regardless of her own wishes and feelings. She felt that she was whole only when she was with him. The attention he gave her made her willing to put up with any degree of degradation and humiliation.

In high school Lynnette continued to develop as a codependent. She was very sexual with the boys and had few or no boundaries. She had never learned how to make real friends and thought that the only way she could get boy to like her was through sexual favors. She began going out and getting drunk, hoping to make her peers think that she was cool and acceptable.

Although Lynnette's father often picked her up after her "dates," her never seemed to notice when she was drunk. Looking back, she believes that he was aware of her problem, but did not know how to handle it and chose to ignore it. In reality, she was involved in a very serious and potentially dangerous lifestyle, drinking heavily and having sex with multiple partners, sometimes partially against her will. When Lynnette met her first serious boyfriend, he introduced her to drugs and she began using with him regularly, sometimes stealing to get money to pay for her habit.

Soon after this, Lynnette got into trouble at school and had to change to a different school. By this time she was addicted to methamphetamines and relied on relationships and drugs to fill the emotional void she had felt since childhood.

After failing an entire semester of school, Lynnette gave up all pretense and began hanging out on the streets, using drugs, smoking and trading sexual favors for money or drugs. Soon she stopped coming home and began living on the streets. The first time she failed to come home, her parents called the police, but after that they let her go. It seemed that they had given up on their daughter. According to Lynnette, when she did go home, her parents ignored her, never acknowledging that she had a problem, although she was still quite young.

Lynnette describes her life during this time, "I became homeless by my own choice. I would sleep with men to get what I needed, and I lived on and off with my ex-boyfriend. I found myself shooting up in rain gutters. I had three psychotic episodes and soon just flat out couldn't get high anymore. I was just using to keep my eyes open and my brain from shutting down. I hated myself, I thought I was worthless, and if I wasn't worth anything to myself, how could anyone else love me? Sex was love. Drugs were love. Any attention was love."

One day she realized the state that her life was in and decided that she needed to make a change. She went to her parents' house and waited for them to come home. When her mother came in, Lynnette forced her to sit down and listen to what she had to say. She described the type of life that she had been living, being totally honest with her mother for the first time. Then she told her that she wanted to stop living this way and was determined to do so, whether her parents would help her or not. Although she was willing to make changes in her life on her own if necessary, Lynnette told her mother that she would like her help. Lynnette's mother called her father and they had a family discussion. It was difficult for all of them to open up and speak to each other after so many years of bottling up their emotions and ignoring the problems in their family. However, that discussion was the starting point for forgiveness and for healing. Lynnette's parents promised they would stand behind her if she would just let them know what they needed to do. They finally recognized that their daughter had a voice worth listening to and they stood behind during her recovery process. By setting and enforcing limits, Lynnette's parents conveyed the message that she was important to them and that her actions mattered.

She describes the difference this has made in her life: "It's been a lot of work. A lot of white knuckling, but now I'm not searching blindly for that something I think I'm missing. I've found it in recovery. I've graduated high school and will start college in the fall. I want to get a counseling degree, and I even have partial scholarships because of my excellent grades in the last two years. I'm going somewhere, and it's not down, for a change."

Bailey tells a story of early abuse, codependency and recovery: "When I was growing up, I was abused. Any form of abuse you can think of, I've been through it. I was a good looking guy, but I never saw it. I thought I was useless, worthless, ugly. My parents complimented me when they were sober and abused me when they were not. I never knew what was going to happen when I came downstairs every day, and most days I didn't want to leave my bed. I wanted their approval, and as I grew older, all my energy was put into getting approval from family, friends and girlfriends.

"Looking back on that, I recognize that my codependency began at a very early age, and that for me it was based on a fear of bad things happening to people I loved. And we didn't discuss our emotions or even display them much. Even to appear too happy was to appear giddy and frowned upon. So I learned to withhold my emotions, never showing anger or pain, never talking about fears and frustrations.

"My codependence was not particularly noticeable to me or to others until my son became an addict and all my worst fears were triggered. I felt an obsessive desperation to save him, doing everything I could think of to save him. For many years I enabled him, thinking that if he could live in a loving home, and if I could control his whereabouts and money that he would be okay. I knew nothing of addiction. When he finally admitted using crack and went to his first program (a thirty-day out-patient program), I thought that after thirty days our lives would be perfect again. I was so very wrong and didn't listen to counselors who tried to explain relapse and the struggle that can go with addiction. I just felt that they didn't know my son.

"I reached my bottom one night when I went to the crack house to get my son to leave. When they wouldn't let me in, saying he wasn't there, I threatened to kick down the door (totally out of character for me and totally insane). He did come out and I spent the night at his place, and when I left the next day he resumed his using. I knew then that I was about to break and lose my mind.

"So I reached out and went into group therapy and met a man there, who is now my sponsor, who had been through the same pain and he was sane, peaceful and strong. I could see that he had something I wanted—serenity. Going to meetings, working the steps, and furthering my recovery has brought me out of the darkness and into the light. I have never felt such joy as when I found my own spirituality and connected with God's plan for me. It's been a long journey, and I have overcome many obstacles along the way and will encounter more I am sure, but today I wouldn't change my life with anyone. The pain that brought me to this program is the greatest gift I have ever been given. Without the pain I would never have found what I have today—a happy, healthy life full of joy and beauty. And my life is beautiful. I have replaced anger with compassion and have a good relationship with my son (albeit with many bumps along the way) and I am free—thank you God. The friends I have found have walked with me every step of my journey, held me up when I could no longer stand, cried with me, and taught me to laugh again, most of all at myself. I am forever grateful."

Charlotte opens up about her step-by-step journey to emotional health, "I couldn't wait to grow up. I couldn't wait to get out of my house. I was never happy with anything about me. I was too fat, too thin, too ugly, too stupid. I kept waiting to blossom and become perfect like all the girls at school, but it never happened. I wanted to be something special but it never happened. I started drinking at about fifteen. My parents were pretty protective, so I didn't get many opportunities to drink, but I loved what alcohol did for me. I was able to talk to people, I was better and everything and I was comfortable with myself. I didn't hate myself as much, and I thought that everyone liked me when I was wasted. I was funnier and smarter and prettier. The only thing that mattered was what others thought of me. My happiness depended on others being happy with me. Drinking helped. When I did get the opportunity to drink, I never knew when to stop. Alcohol gave me the courage to do the things I wanted... and didn't want to do. It became my crutch.

"I got pregnant right out of high school and had a baby at nineteen. I got married to one of those kids I hated from public school. Looking back, I think I did this to prove that I could fit in and that I was good enough. He turned out to be an alcoholic, although he refused to admit it. I worked constantly and tried hard to meet the responsibilities of the family. My parents taught me that if I worked hard, I could have anything I wanted. And in my unhealthy emotional state I thought that that meant a marriage could work if I worked hard enough at it. I had two more children in that marriage. I drank very little during the seven years I was married to this man. But when I did drink, I didn't know when to stop. It was such a relief once I finally worked up the courage to leave.

"I dove into what was ahead of me and focused on my kids. They had private music lessons, baseball, hockey, cub scouts and brownies... all the good stuff. I was involved in all the activities. But I was miserable, angry and resentful. Unfortunately my kids took the brunt of these feelings. I would feel a bad mood coming on and I could not control it or stop it, it just came out and everyone around me paid the price. I always felt guilty and remorseful after, but I didn't understand what was going on.

"I met another guy, older, thought maybe this would work. He always had a bottle of booze and a joint to smoke each night. I soon became a weekend drinker and had a joint every night. Then I started drinking after the kids went to bed. Just enough to relax me. This relationship lasted about two years, but by then I was drinking almost daily.

"One summer my kids were going on a very long trip: it took us two years to raise the money to send them. By this time I was working full time, still had hockey, baseball and everything else going on. I really don't know how we did it, but we did. The weekend I took them to the airport, my brother had promised to watch the younger children; I went home and cried for two days. I couldn't figure out what was wrong other than my life was a mess. I decided that I was going to spend the extra time I had that summer to find the right guy with whom to spend my life."

Looking back, Charlotte realizes that it probably did not matter who she met; she was just looking for someone to fill a void in her life. As it turned out, she met another alcoholic and drug addict. Still, she told herself that if she could only work hard enough and be good enough, he would have to love her and change his ways. When this didn't work, she found herself drinking with him instead, trying to escape her own emotions.

Charlotte very quickly went into a decline and tried to commit suicide three times in a two month period. She was on the verge of losing her job and her children had been taken away. Her life was a mess, but she continued to deny that she had a real problem, even when she went for counseling. Although she was gradually improving, she still suffered from low self-esteem and continued to let her boyfriend disrupt her life and the progress she had made

The breakthrough in Charlotte's life came when she went to a few open AA meetings with boyfriend. For the first time, she really related to what she was hearing. She is still thankful that her boyfriend came into her life and got her into recovery, despite later events. Her recovery process was slow and difficult. She remembers feeling that she was just sick and tired of the way things had been and that there had to be a better way to live. She started really to listen at the meetings she attended and achieved three months of sobriety before she broke down and drank. Then she made it through eight months of sobriety before she drank. Finally, she decided enough was enough and she was going to stop drinking for good. She read all she could about recovery, worked hard and listened to everyone. By this time she had her children back and had bought a house. Her relationship with her boyfriend, however, was still unstable. She wanted him to leave, but did not know how to enforce this wish. He would leave, but he always came back, knowing exactly what to say to persuade her to take him back.

Charlotte's codependent relationship finally came to an end when her boyfriend met an ex-girlfriend and decided to get back together with her. He still attempted to use Charlotte whenever he needed something, but she had finally had enough and told him so. After that, her recovery began in earnest. She recognized that it was time to work on herself and got very serious about recovery, going to meetings every day.

Charlotte tells about the changes that she made in her life after that point: "Things finally started to work for me. I was changing. I decided I was ready to meet someone. I signed up for a date line through a radio station. I got a few calls, but those men weren't for me. Then I got a call from a guy who sounded strong but gentle and we hit it off really well. We had a lot in common and talked everyday. After three weeks of talking we decided to meet. We started seeing each other and got along so well. I thought I was in heaven. He treated me very well. He was good with my kids. He was dedicated to his own kids but the relationship didn't work out.

"Nevertheless, that summer was the best for my recovery. I did things I never thought I could do. My life is so good right now. I didn't get what I wanted from the relationship, but I grew stronger, more independent, for the first time in my life. I did my fourth and fifth, then my six and seventh steps. You out there struggling with being codependents—keep trying. I have found that this program and the people in it are right for me. You will see your own promises come true if you find and work at a program. I didn't think it would happen to me, but it did.

"Life still isn't a bowl of cherries, but I know I don't have to pick up a drink to deal with it. I don't have to carry old garbage around, and I have a choice of how I want to feel about things. It won't happen overnight. It took a long time to get where I was and it will take a long time to recover. But I now know how to live sober and have fun."

Through my research, I've met the most wonderful and courageous men and women, people that make me pray to be a better, stronger woman and mother. By far the person that's had the greatest impact on me is Barb. She is truly one to look up to and proof that we can all make it no matter our childhood. No abuse, no bullying, no stereotypes, no nothing can keep us from being in control ourselves and our surroundings. Barb was put in contact with the local sexual assault center and then a counselor. To her, Barb revealed that she had been sexually assaulted by her own brother and that her father had been physically abusive and an alcoholic. One incident of his drunkenness she told about was especially chilling.

"It didn't take long for him to figure out that my mother was hiding in my room. He came into my room with a hot cup of coffee in his hand and he backed my mother up against my bed and slapped the heck out of her and spilled hot coffee on me. I jumped up after he hit my mother and shoved him as hard as I could into my stereo. It took him a while to get up. I then ran to get my other brother up to help. Then I went back to protect my mother from being hit again. My dad by this time had got up and came in the hallway and slapped my face. We then went to my sister's house for the rest of the night. My mom asked me to go get the loaf of bread off the table at home so we could fix sandwiches at my sister's house and when I got home my dad was at the table and he told me he was going to get me for shoving him into the stereo.

"My dad's drinking didn't seem so bad to me, because I was being sexually assaulted by my brother while all the other stuff was going on. I don't think I can ever get it all told because I always remember something else."

Barb was also sexually assaulted by a cousin.

"He was a mean person. He would scare me with snakes, hit, slap me and pull my hair. One time we went to their house and he caused me to bleed. I got scared because I had never had a period and I didn't know what to do if I was bleeding. I waited until we got home and then I called my mother to the bathroom and she thought I had just got my first period. I didn't tell her that I was hurt and that is why I was bleeding. I was too scared to tell her. I didn't think she would believe me and that I would get the blame for it.

"The worse thing he did was when we all went to my grandparent's house. My cousin was there and he told me he wanted to show me something. I said okay and he said you can only see it from the bathroom window. I said okay. What a stupid person I was. My grandparents' bathroom was huge. As you went in the door the sink and mirror were on the left and the shower and then you walked down like a long hallway to the toilet and the window was at the very end of the room. As soon as I went in the bathroom with him he locked the door and told me to go to the window so I did and then when he got down there he started telling me what he wanted me to do and I told him NO and he said you are going to do it. I said NO and then he put his hands around my neck and started choking me.

"He forced me to perform oral sex on him. I hated him. I think I hated myself for allowing myself to get in such a situation. I was sick. I wanted to cry. I wanted him to die. I was thinking how am I going to get out of this and thank God that my aunt knocked on the door and he stopped and he made me answer her. He told me to tell her that I would be out in a few minutes. He told me if I told that he would hurt me really bad next time. He hid in the shower to make sure that my aunt wasn't at the door when I went out. I waited a few minutes and he came out. Then I went and told my aunt that she could go to the bathroom. I was so glad when we moved, because then we didn't see them that much and every time I would see them I made sure I stayed away from him because I knew if he could get me alone he would do awful things to me like before."

Though moving helped Barb to get away from her cousin, her brother still abused her.

"My mother was in denial that the incest took place. One time I tried to tell my mother and she said she was hoping there was at least one virgin in my family and she wouldn't talk to me. That statement cut me so deep. I started crying. One day after I got off of work

I guess my mother had been thinking about me telling her that my brother raped me and as soon as I walked in the door she told me to tell my brother what he did to me. I told her that I didn't need to tell him because he knew what he did. She proceeded to tell him what I said he did to me and then he said you must have been f-ing dreaming. I said to him you don't dream something like that. I told him you know you did that. He came in the living room where I was and slapped my face. My mother jumped up and told him he had better not hit me again. She told him if he needed to hit anyone again he had better hit her and for him not to put his hands on me again. I was in shock. I told my mother that she had better kick my brother out or I was leaving. I went and got in my car and I drove myself back to my job. I felt like I was going to pass out while I was driving back to my job. I just prayed for God to let me make it back there. A woman I worked with drove me to her house till I got calm enough to go get my car and drive back home.

"Eventually my brother went to jail on other charges. Taking drugs, smoking pot, hitting a few lines of cocaine or shooting it up in his veins. If you don't think living with someone like that will drive you nuts, well, you are wrong. Sometimes he would get so screwed up on all those drugs he was taken he would start talking all kinds of crazy stuff like, 'do you want me to slap you?' or he would pull out a knife and say, 'Let me cut you' or, 'Do you want me to cut you with my knife?' He would threaten to kick my dad's ass. He would yell at my mother all the time about giving him his money. He didn't have any money, because he didn't work. I hated living there.

"I got married to Carl. I didn't plan things out as I should have so we moved in with my mom and dad and the rest of the family. This wasn't a very good idea. Before the week was out my brother went off in one of his rages and my husband didn't know what to think of this behavior. It wasn't good. My marriage has suffered a great deal. For now my husband doesn't know how to handle the abuse I went through. I thought he was okay, but it turned into a huge mess. My husband began trying to protect everyone from my brother. My husband got angry at me for having anything to do with my family. He would take his anger at my family out on me. It got so bad that we moved. I silently cried myself to sleep at night. I was in so much pain. My heart was broken into thousands of pieces and I didn't know how to fix it. I thought after we moved my mother could get away from my brother as well. That did not happen. I started sinking into a deep depression and didn't realize that was what I was doing. I could not function. All I wanted to do was sleep all the time. I had no energy at all. I got my days and nights mixed up. I would sleep all day and stay up all night. For a long time I practically never saw daylight because I went to bed just before the sun came up and woke up right after it went down. All I saw was darkness. I hated the way that made me feel.

"I was pregnant and had to have an emergency c-section. My son was born with internal blockages and a heart problem. The doctor came to me to tell me that they were sending him to a children's hospital. I didn't get to hold him. They rolled him into my room and I was able to put my hand on him for a minute before they left. He was two days old when they did the surgery to correct the intestinal blockage. He was four days old before I was able to leave the hospital and go see him. When I got to the children's hospital and to the ICU where my son was, the nurses wouldn't let me hold him, but when his doctor came in he told them to put him in my arms. He stayed in the hospital three months before I could bring him home with special care. My son was almost two years old and my mother got really sick, she had diabetes and she lost most of her eye sight. She caught pneumonia, had a stroke and then got the shingles. She died of conjunctive heart failure, seven days after my son's birthday.

"My brother has been in and out of mental hospitals and jail countless times for drugs and theft. Being sexually assaulted affects the rest of your life. The mental cruelty that I have to go through because I am reminded of the sexual abuse I went through with him is not fair to me at all. People feel sorry for my brother now, because he has had carbon monoxide poison and they think he is mentally retarded or something because it affected his speech so he talks with a heavy slur. He uses that to do his criminal acts and gets away with it. He never has been charged as a sexual offender. I know that I'm not the only one he did this to. It takes people who have been assaulted and that have been threatened to keep silent about the abuse they went through a very long time to come to terms with the matter. Why should we have a limited time to get something done to our perpetrators, while they can keep going and doing the same things and get away with it? We should be allowed to voice what happened to us when we find the courage to stop being afraid and we have enough support to help us make it through our healing.

"I'm not sure if I will ever not be afraid of my brother. When I see him he always gives me a cold dead stare. He is a very, very sick person. I am in the healing process now. I had totally blanked out a lot of my abuse but since I have been seeing a counselor I have remembered a lot more. I said to myself *I don't want to remember anymore* when I remembered that I had been fondled by two more people. It is best to get it all out even though it doesn't feel so great at the time. It feels like acid running through your veins. You just want the pain to go away but it is there lingering, making your life miserable. It feels like your heart is cut into a million pieces and it is bleeding out of control and you are doing all that you can do to mend all those pieces together to make it whole again. You feel weak in the knees. You feel sick to you stomach. You feel out of control.

"I have blamed myself, I have been ashamed of myself, angry all the time. I've inflicted pain upon myself by cutting my arm, burning myself and doing other things to try to relieve the hurt I felt inside. I've cried countless tears for years and I still cry. However, I feel I have come a long way. My counselor has helped me more than she will ever know. She has let me know that it is okay to cry in front of people if I need to. She has tried to help me see instead of always hitting that wall just open that door and go through it. She has given me lots of encouragement, which I will always be thankful for. She has helped me find some of my inner strength. She has helped me see that I do matter and that I am a lot stronger than I give myself credit for. I am also thankful for my doctor. I am thankful that God put my best friend in my life. She has stayed by my side through some of the roughest times. She has given me a lot of encouraging words and has been very supportive. She helped me a lot in my healing process.

She always gives me a lot of encouragement and assured me that I would one day be able to have a happy life. I know my faith in God has helped me make it to this point in my life and without him I am nothing."

Barb's wish is that her story will help encourage someone who wants to begin to heal. Some people may feel that they are so damaged by their experiences that there is no hope for them, but Barb's story and the other stories in this chapter show that healing and recovery are possible. All you have to do is give yourself permission to put yourself first, then persevere in your commitment to change for the better. These stories of people who have struggled and triumphed in their journeys from codependence to independence and strength will, I hope, inspire you on your own journey. I wish for each of you a destination of hope and joy. Godspeed.

◀ 13 ▶

Recovering and Moving On

I'm at least third generation dysfunctional. But I'm getting better; I know I am. Today I can walk by the pool, by gorgeous, young, skinny bodies without feeling rage and self-hatred. I can stand in my closet and not cry when I look at all my "skinny" clothes that will never again rise above my ankles. I still can't bring myself to throw them away... that's how I know I have a long way to go. While I don't obsess that my boyfriend is looking at girls when he leaves the house without me, I still get a twinge whenever we pass a good-looking gal and his head cricks in that direction. I can't bear it; I don't think I will ever get over that, that feeling of being unworthy. But I'm getting better. I can remember days in the beginning of our relationship where I would rearrange my whole schedule to pop in at his work to "see what the new girl looked like," or got out of the house on a night when I felt like relaxing just to make sure he didn't flirt with another girl while out with his brother. So sad, how insecure I am. But I'm getting better; I know. When I feel the twinge, I tell myself that I'm strong. I've overcome the worst and come through with flying colors. I was like you, a codependent. Now I'm becoming a whole person who can give realistically and expects to be treated as an equal.

I've become a teacher in a poverty-stricken neighborhood where I serve children who really need me. Yes, I'm broke, but I feel useful and important to them. My children are wonderful, intelligent and beautiful. They are both in enriched and honors classes, making great grades. They are well rounded, play sports and music, and love me. Every day I try to make them feel good about themselves, accentuate the positive and don't give a damn about the negative. I love that GoGo's lyric, which is written on my son's school wall, "Pay no mind to what they say; it doesn't matter anyway." That is it; that's the best advice I can give to you, your kids, myself, anyone and everyone who'll take the time to listen. From wherever you are right now when reading this, whether mid-fall or lost between a rock and a hard place, you can start fresh from this point. You have to set priorities and my priorities and yours may be completely different. Both our priorities are to be respected.

If you are ready to take steps toward a healthy lifestyle with another person or just towards healthy self-esteem, write down a list of what you absolutely want. Then write down a list of things you absolutely don't want. Take much time to write both lists. The things you write down on both of these lists are non-negotiable items. So, go over them and make sure these are things that are important to you. For example, if you want to find a man with whom you can have a satisfying, fulfilling relationship and you've dated men in the past who have had certain issues or traits that have broken up the relationship or contributed to its breakup, then consider these things heavily. And spend just as much time writing down what you want and not just the things you don't want.

The whole point of this exercise, whatever your goals, is for you to realize YOU are doing the choosing and that you have this right. Re-read this from time to time to see how you are doing.

Make a list of pros and cons when you begin or continue seeing a new man or woman. Compare this list with your original one. Be matter-of-fact with yourself; lay out your standards. You are your top priority.

Also make two lists of positive and negative traits regarding any person who was abusive in some way to you in the past. You will want to do this especially if the person who abused you was a family member. What you want to have before you at all times is an outline of what you might be drawn to in selecting a partner and what you need to stay away from. You might write down things like, she was a charmer, could be very outgoing and convincing, but it didn't last, had a bad temper, had a substance addiction of some kind, hated her father, had a history of not treating the men in her life well, etc., etc.

Try your best to assemble a list that will sketch this person out for you on paper, so you can recognize what you are doing as you go along. Add to this as time goes on. The more you are aware of what you're doing, the quicker you will have a healthy relationship.

Because we are creatures of resolution, women often will pick men that resemble the abuser in order finally to "fix" it. We then think we will win by being the reason they change for us. We think by doing this we can finally "earn" their approval and love for us or that we can make them pay somehow by doing a dysfunctional dance with us.

This kind of "resolving" is like going back to what originally hurt you and asking for it again! So, whether we realize it or not, we are ending up with particular men in our lives because we may be subconsciously choosing them. By "projecting" someone else's identity onto this present person in our lives we play a very dangerous game that resolves nothing. It only prolongs the pain we are in from the original abuse. The key here is to be aware of who we are being drawn to and why. Keep yourself in check. Learn how to parent yourself in this way. Blinders off, eyes open.

When you first meet a new potential partner, allow yourself to ask the question—is there mutual interest here, or am I so attracted to this person that I will "make" him or her have an interest in me? Try to steer away from situations like this. You don't need to put yourself in a position of having to earn anyone's interest or affections. This will only end in disaster. A potential mate needs to be genuinely drawn to you, without you jumping through any hoops at all. Codependents get into the mode of thinking they have to earn the right to be in someone's life. The thing we have to keep ever before us is that we are the ones doing the choosing. So, write yourself a note and stick it on your refrigerator, in the bathroom and in your car—if you have to—to remind yourself. We need to choose and go about the process decisively, looking at all the ingredients mentioned here. So, breathe... get your focus geared more toward what you are looking for and not what you can become for them. You are not damaged goods and have a right to have the very best, tailor suited just for you. Look deeper than the surface. And look beyond the infatuation: take note of the wonderful feelings, but learn to look at what's really there, in substance. Train yourself to get in order to protect yourself. We may be wired to make wrong choices, but we can "unlearn" our compulsions and override them with wisdom. Quick decisions lead to train wrecks. Go slow... make them "court" you. You don't need to settle for anything less. You are worth it, so act like it!

When contact is made and a conversation begins with a person in whom you're interested, do not "tell all" about yourself in the first sitting. There may be a strong compulsion to do this, but try hard to refrain. Do a lot of listening and observing. Give yourself permission to ask questions of the other person, more than you volunteer very personal information about yourself. Again, have questions prepared... things you think are important to know about someone before you spend serious time together. Sharing some surface information is obviously okay, but not about your deepest hurts. Word to the wise here: do not give anyone that hasn't earned your trust information about where your weaknesses are. Then they will know precisely where to hurt you.

Remember, it is okay if there are silences in your conversation. You don't need to try and fill them with chatter or opinions. You are looking to see if this person you are with is someone who meets the requirements on your two lists—BEFORE your heart gets too involved. Very important concept. Trust is earned and your personal information should be kept confidential for quite a while. It is not necessary to give him the keys to your castle and or to take her to your innermost chambers right away. Otherwise, you may be letting a wolf into the hen house, even though he is a cute wolf who's charming, even though she is a minx and seems like she can't wait.

If you have a history of codependence your brain now needs to rule supreme or lessons will be presented in life to learn once again (and again and again) as the price of these lessons gets higher and higher. Time is always a very good friend... back off, listen, learn and don't reveal yourself too quickly.

Watch how he treats you or she acts on the first date. Is he or she sincerely attentive? Or is he or she overly flattering, concentrating largely on the physical aspects? Does he or she try to get into your personal space too soon? Does the person have a real two-way conversation with you? Does the person listen to you as much as he or she talks to you and about him- or herself? Is he or she constantly scanning the room and checking out others? Monitor how comfortable you feel with this person. Learn to listen to your radar and what your impressions are. They are very important. Try not to override them, but bring them to the forefront and turn the volume up so you can really pay attention to it.

Those of use who have abuse issues often have a radar that has sustained a lot of damage, and that little voice inside can be small and frail. Nonetheless, we must listen to it. We are used to accepting anything or trying to work with anything we get thrown, almost as if we take it as a challenge of some sort to bypass all the warning lights and try and just—MAKE IT WORK, DAMMIT!! We don't have to do that. We can pick someone who doesn't set off the alarm system at all or very rarely. It isn't necessary to run a marathon obstacle course in order to get what we deserve and need.

Try very hard not to get hot and heavy in the physical department right away. This is especially good advice for men who are with women who have been abused and taken advantage of in the sexual area in the past. It may feel good and natural and all that, but it does put you in an extremely vulnerable position. It will cloud your perception of all the other things you need to be paying close attention to. You also need to "really feel" what's going on and not just do something because it "seems natural." So what if it takes you longer to really feel it? Don't overcompensate. Don't push the envelope. You may just push it over the edge and out of sight!

If this happens anyway, back off, set a boundary about it and go from there. There's nothing wrong with that. Your partner needs to respect that and if he or she doesn't, don't waste your time. If you are going to give yourself in a physical way, it needs to be when you feel like you really know this person and are really able to trust him or her. Otherwise, it will backfire on you; count on it. And there will be repercussions.

I firmly believe that when a physical union happens, there is an uncanny thing that takes place. I think the woman immediately leans into the man and the man leans over the woman. It's a beautiful design. The woman wants to be cared for by the man and he feels protective and wanting to take care of her, too. Or at least, this is the way it should be.

Many women's hearts become majorly engaged with the physical act whether we want them to or not. Many men like the chase and the mystery, but their hearts need to be involved too. The hurt inflicted can be very expensive to you both, especially if you have a codependency problem. Take your time. Learn about the other person. Otherwise, you'll be so wrapped up in the sexual, you'll never even notice important attributes that will tell you whether this is a positive or another negative union. Sex should be an expression of love that has had proper time to grow, not the reason and basis for love. There is a big difference between lust and love. Love takes time. Be good to yourself here. Be your own best friend.

Find out how long the other person's last relationship lasted and how serious it was. Try to ascertain if he or she is over that relationship break-up. Depending on how serious it was and what kind of break-up was involved, the time frame of space between them and you will vary. The proper amount of time needs to be there in order for the person truly to be available for a new relationship of any kind. Otherwise, you open yourself up to residual feelings from his or her last relationship and you may even end up sharing the person in a sense while he or she cleans up dealings with an old flame. This is not a healthy beginning for a relationship and most do not survive such a strain in the long run. Look carefully before you leap. Be forewarned. If you are the person recently involved, take the time to really do some purging and get back into that space of being comfortable with yourself and being alone for a while—a very healthy thing for anyone to do, male or female.

If you've been part of a codependent relationship and are now on the verge of commitment, it isn't necessary for you to have everything in common, but it is necessary that you have some very important places of common ground. These important areas usually fall into the categories of lifestyle, age, morals/ethics, spiritual matters, intellect, family issues and activities. Write down and then review these areas carefully with yourself as you're getting to know the other person. If you're coming from opposite ends of the spectrum on most or all of these things pause to reflect about what you're getting into. Your togetherness should never be all about his or her world or all about yours. You need to have a blending of who you both are.

What you are checking out in the beginning is whether or not a blending can occur. When one person always yields to the other person's persuasions, activities, thinking, there will be a serious imbalance. Both people should show sincere interest and respect for what the other person is about. Tolerating just isn't enough of a basis on which to form a positive relationship.

Ask yourself what you see in this man or woman that makes the person attractive to you, besides the physical. Write down your ideas and answers. Keep looking at them as time goes on. Add or delete and see how the list changes as things develop. Be accountable to yourself in this way and be very honest. Writing this down helps you not to do dysfunctional things. It brings things out into the light and out of the hypnotic state we so often get into during the beginning of a relationship.

Reality will come knocking sooner or later so it would be in our best interest to see the freight train and jump off the tracks before it hits us. If you choose a partner who already has qualities you want, then you are ahead. At the start of a relationship ask yourself if you are overlooking a lot of faults and centering on a charming picture you've sketched in your head of this person.

Beware of the person who tells you that you are his or her everything! Anyone who tells another person that is putting tremendous pressure on the other individual right away. You are so much their everything that you are also held responsible if this perfect vision they have in their heads gets blurred for some reason. This is a scary situation that entices and breeds codependent personalities. And it sounds oh so wonderful! Don't get me wrong; I know how great it sounds. Boosts up your ego, strokes everything you've got and pumps you up! Well, the fall from that high pedestal smarts. Basically, this controlling individual is putting your name on the dotted line for being responsible for how his or her life goes. And if something doesn't go well then you're the one blamed. Never assume this position again. It's one thing for someone to express how much you mean to him or her and to say that you complement his or her life wonderfully. But to state early on how your presence in the person's life just solves everything wrong with his or her life and the person can't make it without you, you're all he or she has ever dreamed of, etc., etc.—look out! It may feel good to be supposedly so important. But that "importance" can change very quickly and the person usually becomes very demanding as time goes on.

You won't be able to keep up. The controller will suck you dry. You both need to be able to stand on your own two feet and have "completeness" in yourselves without anyone else.

The significant other you choose should enrich your life more, not be the sole reason for your existence. Controllers are good salesmen, but in the end they take that pedestal apart a piece at a time and you with it.

If you are a recovering codependent with a budding new relationship, ask yourself if you are you able just to be alone together and have quiet time. Look at the dynamics in your new relationship early on. Being able to sit in silence with someone and not feel like you have to fill up that space with anything is a very important attribute of building a good relationship. It shows how relaxed a person is with him- or herself. Talking and activity are important things. But so is quiet time. People who are emotionally healthy don't feel threatened by silence. There are many ways of communicating with someone, such as when a person feels hurt. Trying to talk to the person isn't always the answer. Neither is talking at the person! The best thing can be to just sit with him or her and respect the silence. He or she will talk when ready. Sometimes, you have to earn your right to be close to someone by knowing when to shut up and just be with them. And it doesn't have to be a sexual interlude either. We can communicate on another level of intimacy. Former codependents need to learn this.

If you find yourself continuously preaching to the other person in your life about things that you don't like, this is destruction, not relationship building. Wanting this person to change for you down the road or taking the position that you will just deal with these big differences is putting yourself in the place of victim all over again. The other person shouldn't be in the position of clay that you need to mold either. That's not fair to them either. Turning from doormat to controller is not a positive pattern.

Communication is an issue former codependents need to work hard to improve. You have to, have to, *have to* express in an appropriate, non-inflammatory way how you feel when things come up that bother you in some way. There is a big difference between preaching and expressing your feelings about issues. One is wanting to change someone and the other is about expressing yourself and not holding things in. One is attacking and the other is simply stating how you feel. What you want to find out when stating your feelings is how you are received. Does this person truly consider your feelings and discuss things in a non-combative way? Basically, does he or she give you respect? Or does the person ignore what you said, say something that completely invalidates you and shuts you up? Don't walk away just stuffing those feelings back down and not being heard. Take a step back. Maybe the other person was having a bad day, so try it again. However, don't keep making excuses. If this becomes a pattern, then it's obvious your feelings don't matter. Arguments over this kind of thing don't solve one thing. See it for what it is and go the other direction. Again, don't try to browbeat the other person or nag him or her until the person changes to suit you. Look at what is there and make a decision that is good for you. This doesn't have to involve a process of quarreling and trying to get someone to understand something over and over again. Don't beat the subject to death or beat someone into submission about anything.

Watch the other person's actions and don't pay so much attention to his or her words. Apply this big concept to the decision-making process in your life. All of us are so vulnerable to con artists and charmers. Do not remain with a partner whose words do not line up with his or her actions. Give yourself the time to see the pattern emerge. Listen to the nice words... and then wait to see what life prints out. That is the real truth. If someone needs to tell you so much about how great he or she is in a relationship and how good he or she will be to you, methinks he or she doth protest too much. The people that will really do all that won't talk about it. They'll just do it. And you need to be okay with waiting for that to evolve over time. Women and men fall for charmers. Just because a person doesn't go on and on doesn't mean he or she won't be a good mate. It may mean that he or she is not a phony! Sometimes, we might even feel like we're bored with someone who isn't a charmer. This is something to be addressed, because it will lead us to nothing but heartache. It is possible to arrive at a place of being able to recognize a good man or woman when you see one. You just have to be willing to learn what a good person consists of.

Here are some important questions to ask yourself: Does the person listen to the things you say and later let you know that he or she remembers? Does he or she pay attention to the things that matter? Does the person give to you emotionally, going out of his or her way for you? Or does the person only go out of his or her way for you when trying to get you to do something? Are you seeing your potential partner give to you in an unconditional way, just because he or she cares? If you do not see this kind of giving from the other person, you are on a one-way street. Look out for the Mack truck, because it's coming. Don't assume the other will care later down the road when that person hurts you, because he or she won't. Too many times we ignore the signals until it's too late. We do all the giving and the caring and they just charm us when they need us. A charmer/abusive personality is very good at letting the good times roll and then treating you like crap, and on and on the cycle goes. We wonder what happened, because we weren't in love with who they really were, we were in love with the fairy tale picture we believed they were. Look at who the man or woman you're seeing really is early on and pay close attention. Do not do all the giving, all the calling, all the understanding and all the caring. The other person will disrespect you for it; he or she will use you up and suck you dry.

More signs to look for: Go beyond employment. Does he or she have a life outside of you? Does the person have a balanced life of outside interests, hobbies, sports, friends and family? He or she doesn't have to be in a whirlwind of activity or anything, but just basically, does the person have his or her own space to retreat to that doesn't include you? And do you have that going on in your life as well? You both need time away from each other and it also shows you whether this man or woman will be making you responsible for his or her happiness. No one needs to smother anyone. It might feel nice at first, but it can definitely wear on you. And can be a really good sign of someone who is very insecure and possessive/jealous. That might feel good to your ego at first, but it can get ugly on both sides of the fence. You both need your lives apart. And neither of you needs to tag along with the other one while the partners do their "other things." Once in awhile is fine, but not all the time. Let there be spaces between you. It's a good thing that makes the appreciation for the relationship grow. No one needs to grow within a shadow of someone else. In that event there will be no growth. Only suffocation.

Family of origin questions to ask: does this person hate his or her mother or father or have some serious unresolved issues with his parents? If so, this is a serious warning sign to you. This will probably impact you more than anything I can think of. People will sometimes not talk about this, but it's important that you find out what's what in this area. The way the person feels towards parents, if he or she hasn't worked through a lot of things, will end up being something you deal with. The same is true if you haven't worked out your issues regarding your father and mother. You'll end up transferring a lot of stuff over to your partner as well. If the person is still involved in a very unhealthy and angry relationship with parent figures, this is a negative portent for your future relationship. It's one thing if he or she stays away from parents because he or she just chooses not to be intertwined with chaos and trauma and has disconnected in a healthy way. It's another if your partner is still engaging to the point of being very mean, or if the parent meddles in his or her life and keeps this vicious cycle going. Some men are involved in a passive aggressive way of dealing with a mother they have issues with, too. They just seem to needle each other back and forth without ever coming right out and being honest with each other. Some women have little or no relationship with their fathers and transfer such feelings to the men in their lives. Whatever pattern of behavior you see here, know that it could be the same one you end up with as well.

Past relationships give clues. What kind of relationships did he or she have with a significant other in the past? It isn't necessary that he or she remain friends with all past partners. Obviously, something wasn't right and didn't work out or your potential partner would still be with that person. However, it is good to analyze what the usual pattern was. You usually pick this up over time and can get a lot of information through other people. Just observe and keep such things confidential. Did she try to work through their differences? Did he just feel like things weren't working and instead of breaking up, did he get involved with someone else before they broke up? How does she talk about these men now? Does he talk about them in a respectful way or in a way that says everything was their fault? And do you see a pattern of your partner realizing his or her own mistakes and working on them? Do you see the person repeating the same mistakes over and over again? What kind of person does he or she usually pick? Does he or she like to be in control? Does he or she want to be controlled?

Is the person one of those men or women who remains friends with most of the people he or she ever dated? If this doesn't bother you, that's fine, but you do need to ask the question of how you feel about this matter. You need to ask yourself why a person would stay so overly invested in with an "ex" in the first place. A lot of people do this in order never to have to go to a real level of intimacy with the person they are with. They are so spread out with all these others that they never seem to have the energy. And they immensely enjoy the attention and being able to talk freely with you about going to a lunch with someone, or so-and-so called me and talked for two hours about needing some advice, or I'm going over to hang out with my ex-husband or wife's family for a while because we are so close. Some of this in moderation wouldn't necessarily be a warning sign. But a person who has a constant diet of this sort of thing might be in the *I'm emotionally unavailable* category. When you get serious with someone, you need to feel like you're the number one priority and not one of many. Don't settle for less.

Problem solving as a character indicator: Does he or she procrastinate when there are problems in his or her own life? Or does the person face it head on, critically think it through, choose a solution, try it, if it doesn't work, go to Plan B? Is he or she a person of follow-through? Or does the person just try to ignore an uncomfortable or bad situation for a while until things get into a critical stage and he or she is forced to do something? How does she deal with other people when there's conflict? Does he respect people and their views, however different from his own? Is she quick to anger? Is his anger appropriate? Or does she react with a lot of anger to little things? And is he or she able to express appropriate anger or discomfort? Most importantly, does he or she take responsibility for his or her own actions? Does the person admit when he or she is wrong? The way he or she problem solves in his or her life will be the way the person solves problems with you when they arise.

Expressing differences of opinion is another important area at which to look. Are you able to disagree with him and feel relatively comfortable doing it? Can you banter back and forth in a constructive way that is respectful of each other? Do you believe that she is truly listening to your side and do you want to listen to hers? Is there a good amount of give and take? Are there spaces in your debate, where you're both just being quiet and thinking about what's been said? Or are there a lot of instant put-downs, which eventually lead to shutdown? Do you come away feeling like maybe you've learned something new or are at least trying to go there? When you tell her about something that concerns you, does she immediately try to fix it? Do you wish he'd just sit there and listen and really hear you? Do you come away from a disagreement thinking about the next way you can approach whatever issue and win? If it's about one-upmanship, good luck. Debating can be positive if it's done right. It's not about winning;

it's about sharing opinions and being open. Each partner can always learn something from any disagreement. A closed mind never learns anything, except how to be a lonely tyrant or be crushed.

Be sure to consider whether your expectations are realistic. When we are "so ready" for a relationship, we tend to do what I call fairy tale thinking. Women especially paint everything with silvery paint and sprinkle glitter all about. Then, when it starts to fade and crumble, we get extremely angry that things didn't work out the way our expectations dictated they should. This isn't fair to the other person and it's certainly not fair to you. You have to recognize what you are doing while you are doing it and want to stop it.

Look at what your expectations really are. Are you wanting this person to "fix" you and to be your "everything?" If so, it won't work. You have to be a whole person before you can seek out another whole person. And that's the only way a healthy relationship is built. If he or she leans on you all the time, things will eventually crumble from the imbalance. Each person comes into the other's life with past history, needs and desires. You have to view that carefully and be aware of it at all times. No one is capable of being a fairy tale hero or heroine. Beware of the person that says he or she can play this role. This is a charmer and a control freak in operation. Make sure you don't do this to your partner as well. Yes, we deserve to be treated well. But we have to make sure we aren't the ones abusing someone else by our expectations. If we don't adhere to this we will sabotage ourselves. The present person in our lives is not responsible for what others did to us in the past.

Does she take an interest in your talents or hobbies? Does he genuinely appreciate what interests you? Many times, I've seen that women are the ones who bend over backwards to support the men in their interests and to brag and be their cheerleaders. But hey, that door should swing both ways. And you don't need to settle for less. However, whatever it is that you are good at and that you are really interested in, she should respect and appreciate you for it and give her support to you. Paying attention to what you do and how much you enjoy it is called caring for the whole person, not just the parts that you want from him or her. Little acts of respect or disrespect in arenas like this will tell you much about how much the other person really does or does not care. It doesn't do any good to yell or nag about it either. Just believe yourself lucky to see it early on and consider its weight, especially when deciding to make it a long term relationship. That's what dating is all about. It's about learning these things before you jump. Not after.

What is an emotionally healthy man or woman? What does he or she look like? Healthy men and women will do a lot of the same things we've mentioned here. Healthy men and women aren't going to require us to perform for them or earn anything. Normal might appear dull, but continue looking... She will be a good listener and won't always have to pound her opinion into your head. He will have good boundaries and will maintain his friendships and outside interests while seeing you. She will consider you when it comes to going places and won't just always take control. She'll ask you what you like and you need to be ready to tell her. He won't be all over you in a physical way. She won't have to persuade you with her sexual side. He can be attracted to other realms of who you are, so please allow for this process to happen. She will only tell you things when she means them and that may take a while to happen. It should take time. If you're used to a lot of things being said early, review these relationships and ask yourself how many of them worked out. Sincere people wait until they really mean it... then they say it. What's real takes time to grow.

As you read through this book, you may have realized that you still have some areas that need attention before you enter another relationship. I encourage you to do just that. Take time out to learn about yourself. Get to know who you really are and what makes you happy. Learning to be alone with yourself and to truly like you and be at peace with yourself may take some doing. But one thing is for sure: if you do not do this, you will make the same mistakes over and over again in your relationships.

If you still have serious codependent issues, get some counseling and choose your therapist well. Check out some self-help books at the library and educate yourself. Get into a support group where you can learn and share with others. If you cannot learn to love yourself, no one else will be able to either.

The road to self-sabotage is paved with people who remain mired down in evasions about their own feelings and past history.

I've been there, done that, and I intimately know your heartache and the depression it causes if you get on this path. From the bottom of my heart, I wish you well and hope that you choose to grow. It's work, but it's worth it. You will learn to celebrate your uniqueness by putting your nose to the grindstone and persevering in self-discovery, so that whether you have assumed the role of doormat or control freak, you will not choose dependency again. Be hopeful. Be diligent. A healthy relationship awaits you.

◀ 14 ▶

12 Steps to Redefining Your Life

I began this book with a wonderful quote from Mahatma Ghandi: "A 'no' uttered from deepest conviction is better and greater than a 'yes' merely uttered to please, or what is worse, to avoid trouble." As true as that is and as much as we'd like to live by that standard, I think a saying by Charlie Brown himself captures our relationship woes best: "Nothing takes the taste out of peanut butter like unrequited love." Saying no, living a fulfilling life and knowing when unrequited love is not healthy are goals we all should seek. But just like you can want a college degree, nothing will happen until you start taking classes. And if you don't take the right classes, you don't arrive at the degree you wanted originally. As with everything in life, there are particular concrete steps that need to be taken to reach your goal of a mature, rewarding partnership and an independent, fulfilling life.

After researching many twelve-step programs I found that for me to regain control of my life I had to formulate and organize my own. I integrated others and added necessary steps. Feel free to be creative when you organize and adopt this twelve-step plan. Add and subtract as necessary in order to reach your goal. I call it Twelve Steps to Independence and Fulfilling Relationships. What we've been doing up to this point in our lives has not been working. Some of us are only slightly off track, others need a compass, GPS and a guide to find our way to a life of independence and a fulfilling relationship.

Twelve Steps to Independence and Fulfilling Relationships

1. Understand your past choices in order to make better—and by better I mean different—ones in the future. You have a right to make mistakes or fall short of your mark; everyone does. However, if you are to create a stronger life and relationship without recurring mistakes and unhealthy situations, you need to understand and study every aspect of your past choices and present relationships. Create a journal. First make a list of what you need to feel satisfied and what you will no longer accept.

2. Research your negative contributions to failed relationships in order to recognize and break destructive patterns. It takes two to create a control freak/doormat relationship. In your journal answer the following: what hurtful things have you and your partner done in this relationship? Has this happened in past relationships as well? Do you see the same patterns with family, friends and past significant others? Be aware that you've got to set boundaries for yourself and for those in your life. In *Dirty Dancing*, gorgeous hunk Patrick Swayze says to ridiculously cute and skinny Jennifer Grey, "This is my space; this is your space. Don't come in my space and I won't go in yours." Make this a goal. You must have your space, your emotional boundaries. You are allowed to become angry and your significant other is entitled to his feelings as well, but the key here is to know that his feelings belong to him and yours belong to you. You are responsible only for your emotions and no one else's. Admit to mistakes and correct them if possible, but do not apologize for things for which you have no responsibility and do not cover up or take responsibility for the errors and shortcomings of others.

    In my past, I've had significant others who got upset with work or home or even football games and turned that anger on me. More than a few times I have hidden in the bathroom, willing myself to become one with the wall, shrinking from the verbal tirade that came from seemingly nowhere while I was minding my own business reading or cooking or some other task. Then, when it was finally over my significant other often left. The result: somehow he felt better and went right back to that damn football game or whatever he was doing when the firecracker lit. And I felt awful, terrified, disgusting. Sometimes my controlling partner didn't leave but lamely apologized. "Baby, I'm sorry. I didn't mean to hurt your feelings. I love you. I was just [mad, angry, pissed off, stressed out, annoyed, scared, whatever]. I feel better now." And I said nothing and stayed in the relationship, fearing the next explosion, which always came.

When there is a visible pattern of interrupted personal space, your relationship is not healthy. There are so many things I could have done to change the destructive relationships I had, things I wish I'd done, the first of which would have been to stand up and say, "Hey, I see you're upset. I did not cause you to be upset. I am not responsible for you being upset. Please, don't hesitate to tell me why you're angry; I'd love to listen to what's bothering you, but we've got to work on your delivery first." I didn't do that in the past. Now I do. You can too. And if I find that I'm angry, in a grumpy mood, when my life or relationship has hit a snag, I give a little disclaimer now. When someone has been harassing me unduly and I walk into my classroom ready to be combatant, I step back and tell my students how I'm feeling. "I'm so sorry. I'm feeling a little grumpy today and I'm not going to take it out on you. Just know that my anger has nothing to do with you. I love you all." Within the hour, I always end up receiving a "We love you, Ms. Lewis" card, which makes me laugh and cry and feel so much better. I do that with my own kids and significant other, too, and, invariably, just sharing helps me along through a day in which I might otherwise have made some poor choices.

Healthy boundaries must be set so that you and your significant other can vent to each other and with each other, but not at each other. The boundaries separate your feelings and emotions from his and vice versa. When you have healthy boundaries, you can recognize when someone is trying to manipulate you. They also allow you not to feel guilty for saying no or refusing to participate in the door-mat scenario. Once you are comfortable with your space, you can become more flexible to fit the situation, but to begin with the lines need to be drawn in black and white. You have a right to put an end to conversations with people who deliberately put you down, lay guilt trips, manipulate or humiliate you. Having your own boundaries also means being able to express all your feelings in non-destructive ways at the right time and in the right place. If someone invades your space, you are justified in leaving immediately with no excuses or further comment. You are only responsible for you. Define your space and make it your safe place. That is a major step to regaining control of your life.

3. Define and redefine your goals. Your first goal, if you are struggling with a codependent relationship, is to change your self-image. Understand that you are "stuck" and only you can step beyond your past solutions that are not working into ones that are more effective. If it's broke, fix it. Next you must learn to communicate effectively, assertively and lovingly. Third you must let go. We must let go of some of our attachments, especially those that are increasing conflicts and squelching our chance for happiness. Your own relationship with your feelings and emotions is the most important one you have. If you do not have a healthy self-relationship, no others will work.

4. Grow comfortable with speaking your mind and showing your true emotions in a healthy, non-combative way no matter the consequences. This is the hardest step for me. I still struggle with being true to myself in work, family and intimate relationships daily, wherever I am. Often in a personal relationship you feel a roller coaster of emotions, high and low. It's easy to share the joyous feelings, but there are others much

more difficult to impart, or at least to impart using the correct communication skills. Some negative feelings that many of us have in relationships are rejection, worthlessness, fear of losing the significant other and never finding another mate, hurt, loneliness, unhappiness, shame, bitterness, resentment, guilt, jealousy, anger, revenge, depression and many, many more. I've felt all of these emotions. Perhaps you have too. They have a whirlwind effect on your physical as well as mental being. Accept that most have felt such emotions at one time or another. And that is okay. What's detrimental is holding onto them until you explode or, worse yet, implode. You have a right to share your feelings and if your significant other is the right one, he or she will listen and share his or her own feelings.

Strengthen communication skills. Most times we don't communicate our personal needs and dislikes in an assertive way or we don't understand what someone else is trying to convey to us. Improving on this means developing good listening skills. I'm reminded of a line from a Simon and Garfunkel song, "Sound of Silence": "People talking without speaking, people hearing without listening." Have you ever been in an argument and while the other person is telling you what is bothering them, you are already formulating your response? Stop doing that! Call your significant other on it too, because more likely than not, while you are shouting your response, he or she is not listening, but formulating his or her own. Have a "wait time" between responses—listen to what the other person is saying and then think about what you are going to say before you say it. This is hard to do in the heat of an argument, when all you want is to get your point across and you couldn't care less about the other person's point. And vice versa.

Communication often becomes an unconscious, automatic pattern that is hard to change. Developing new skills, unlearning the old and lots of practice are necessary to make that change. It's perfectly all right to disagree with your partner, and both parties should feel comfortable in sharing feelings of discomfort without fear of retribution. If you both cannot learn to communicate what you feel in an accepting environment, it's time to move on.

In a partnership it is critical that each member find someone to listen to his or her feelings and emotions, and that you are not interrupted or given advice.

5. Be positive—focus on *cans* instead of *cannots*. Place yourself in situations, jobs and relationships with people who affirm your intelligence, perceptions and self-worth. Avoid situations or people who are hurtful, harmful or demeaning. I have tried to put my psychological background and my personal plan for growth to work in my classroom. We have instituted a project where students take ten can labels and write "I can _____ " on each of them. Throughout the year when they feel badly about something in their lives, we pull out the cans, read the labels and reflect on them. I'm not asking you to do that, although Freud might think this regression therapy would be important. In your notebook, list ten things you are good at—silly things and serious things like telling jokes, sports, education, emotional insights, social skills, whatever. Know that everyone has faults. Some people focus on their faults and others hide them very well. You don't need to do either. I tell my students, "Okay, so you're not so great at math... you are an incredibly good reader and you are funny... you crack me up! And on the playground, I've seen you turn some flips that the other kids envy. So what you need to do is... know that you need to work on math, improve yourself, but know that there are math freaks out there that can't flip at all." The confidence I seek to build in my students I want to impart to you. Rejoice in your strengths and beat your weaknesses. This is a long speech for kids and it never works the first time, but by the time the year is over, they feel good about themselves. They compliment each other when they do well in subjects they are comfortable with and they hoot and holler and cheer when they improve in their weak subjects. Know your strengths, know your

weakness, know that everyone has both. Celebrate your intelligence, strengths and creativity, and remember not to hide these qualities from yourself and others. Let go of shame, guilt and any behavior that keeps you from loving yourself and others.

6. Pain in relationships is inevitable. In love, friendship, family, nothing is perfect. Accept the ups and downs of life as natural events that can be used as lessons for growth. Step away from the Cinderella world you've been living in. Know that in intimate relationships there will be arguments, conflicts and disagreements. Remember always, though, through every painful moment, that although these feelings are strong and feel unending, they will, indeed, pass. No feelings will ever damage or destroy you physically and if they are damaging you mentally, you've got to leave the relationship. If at any time in your relationship the pain becomes unhealthy or physically harmful, it's time to change things around. Learn from the hurtful situations. Observe and recognize them and make decisions about how they can be resolved and avoided in the future. You are not helpless in any situation. Fix it or leave.

7. Find forgiveness for those who've wiped their muddy boots on you. However, there's a fine line between forgiving someone then moving on, and forgiving and letting it happen again and again. What I mean by true forgiveness is learning to understand the actions and reactions that you and significant others in your life have taken in the past. Understanding them does not mean that they were the correct actions, only that you understand where they came from. Perhaps they came out of self-defense, self-preservation, pain or a communication barrier. Perhaps your partner was raised in an environment that taught no other way of conflict resolution. Again, that doesn't make it right, but once you understand where your partner is coming from, forgiveness is possible. Remember: The grass is always greener on the other side, but you still have to mow it. We are all raised in different families with various communication styles or none at all. Then we get together and are expected to mesh as one and that's

not so easy to do. By the time we become significant others, we may have decades of training to unlearn. Not so easy for either side to do. In achieving forgiveness we realize that we are not expected to care *for* others, but to care *about* others. We are not to fix others, but to be supportive of them. We do not regret the past, but learn from it and grow into the future, a stronger person in spite of it. In forgiving, we fear less and love more.

8. Write a letter (or email) to your significant other, friends or family members who've used you knowingly or unknowingly in the past. Whether you send the letter or not is your choice. Once in high school I felt like I couldn't possibly pass this tough history test. History is my weakness. I can ace any math, English or science test without even attending the classes, but I can read a history book and not retain any relevant information. Anyhow, I wore a long T-shirt to school that day and on the bus I turned the bottom of the shirt inside out and wrote all of the answers on it. I felt so guilty; I'm not the cheating type, but I was just so frazzled. When I sat down to take the test, though, I found that the simple act of writing the answers had strengthened the connections in my brain so that I remembered every one of them. I didn't even have to use my cheat shirt. Since then, I retype all of my notes and see that children, of course, do theirs as well. Now this letter is your cheat shirt. Write it; feel it; let it strengthen your willpower. Here's mine:

"Dear_____(fill in the mud-wiper's name here),

"After much soul searching, though I would like you to find happiness in your life, I can't create it for you. Moreover, I know now I don't want to be responsible for your fulfillment when you feel unsatisfied and I don't want you to feel you must do the same for me. I want to focus on the wonderful things I have or can create in my life. I hope you will be able to do the same. I want to try to live without feeling guilty or angry with you because you feel unfulfilled.

"We have had an unhealthy codependence in which we've tried to find self-worth through making each other responsible for our happiness. I hope we'll be able to discuss this and listen to each other. I am going to try to do my part and work on healing myself. I hope you will do yours."

As I said before, whether this letter is sent or kept hidden under your pillow, simply putting your feelings into words is a step toward self-preservation, strength and becoming a healthier you.

9. Find new interests. Find new hobbies, join clubs or groups, make new friends. It's never too late for a second (or third or fourth) chance at life. At well over my desired weight, with no sports experience in my life, I am playing soccer. I am so very bad at it, but I have a blast. I like to tell people, in yet another of my many disclaimers, "The worst sports pain I've had in my life is when I got a paper cut from reading too fast." It's true, but after my divorce I knew I had to get out there, do something healthy, not vegetate miserably in front of the television every evening. Now I am active. I've met a whole new world of people and I can share so much with my kids, who play too. Try something new. Join a book club, a sports team, take a class at the community college, do something positive and new. Tell yourself, as I do, you can do anything! Old dogs can and do learn new tricks. The world is open for you.

10. Take care of the children. There's a good reason that airline attendants tell you to put your oxygen mask on first before putting it on your children. You need to be healthy to take care of your children. You need to present yourself as a strong, rational adult, ready to stand up for yourself in the right way. Just as you and your significant other are using communication skills (or lack thereof) that you learned from your parents, so will your children. What children are seeing on a daily basis is how they will relate with their significant others in the future. If boys see their male role model shouting and screaming, that's what they will tend to do. If girls or

boys see a parent cowering in a corner, never speaking up for him- or herself, or if children see a parent verbally abuse another, then that's what they'll usually view as "normal" relationship communication techniques. Make a choice to shield your children from unhealthy parental conflict. When you learn how to communicate with your significant other, the children should see how mature people resolve conflicts, but even then, be spare in what you let them see. Work hard to explain clearly and directly to children that arguments are not their fault. Children need continuity, structure, routine, consistent discipline, familiarity and mutual respect between parental figures. Never allow children to see chronic conflict; do not speak in negative ways about the other parent or abandon your children physically or emotionally, no matter what you are going through. Now, while you are learning communication and conflict resolution, teach your children the right way to handle problems before they too become doormats or control freaks.

11. Create a support network. Sometimes that means getting a new one! If the same friends keep giving you the same advice, maybe it's time to broaden your horizons. After you follow step 9, you'll have met many new people and will be on your way to making connections with new communication skills in place. You probably can't change old patterns your child-hood family, but you can revamp your relationship with them using the other steps which we've discussed.

12. If you are single or single again, stop searching for a soul-mate. Let it happen naturally. Do not look for a love at first sight. Stop searching for an instantly strong connection, but look for something more deep and abiding. Take your time. Be up front with your new companions, let them know your boundaries regarding sex and intimacy. Become good friends while you date; get to know each other. If the man or woman has a one-track mind and that train is heading to Sexville rather than Emotional Connectionville, ditch this one before you're spinning in circles again. To gain a

fulfilling intimate relationship, establish a standard of communication from the start, one with which you are both comfortable. Accept him or her as the other person must accept you. Be aware you will never do things or see things exactly the same. If the other person's points of view or actions are not what you'd like in a permanent mate, move on. Don't invest energy in trying to change a person, or even worse, staying and trying to change yourself for someone.

Remember and review the boundaries you've set—what you need to maintain your own happiness. Just as you must learn to appreciate the good things about your partner, you must accept his or her shortcomings as well. Remember, no one is perfect. Build a relationship of equals, not codependents, in which neither partner seeks to control or become subservient to the other. Celebrate and accept each partner's uniqueness and freedom to be the best he or she can.

Appendix
Resources for Living

http://www.codependents.org/
Co-Dependents Anonymous is a fellowship of men and women
whose common purpose is to develop healthy relationships. The
only requirement for membership is a desire for healthy and loving
relationships. We rely on the Twelve Steps and Twelve Traditions
for knowledge and wisdom. These are the principles of our program
and guides to developing honest and fulfilling relationships.
Through applying the Twelve Steps and principles in CoDA to our
daily life and relationships, both present and past, we can experience
a new freedom from our self-defeating lifestyles and realize a new
joy, acceptance and serenity in our lives.

http://www.selfesteem4women.com
If you have any issues that you think may be affecting your confidence and self-esteem, then you've definitely come to the right place!
Our unique approach to building women's self-esteem is refreshingly
different, is very easy to follow and has a twelve-year proven track
record of success.

http://www.drirene.com/
This is the place for you if you think you may be in an abusive relationship or may be abusive yourself.

http://alcoholism.about.com/od/coda/

http://www.childabuse.com/
Comprehensive resource bringing awareness and education in preventing child abuse and related issues. Childabuse.com was created to support, inform and encourage those dealing with any aspect of child abuse, in a positive non-threatening environment.

http://www.selfgrowth.com/codepend.html
Codependency, substance/alcohol abuse websites, links on the Internet... Self Improvement Online's Recommended and Reviewed

http://www.recovery-man.com/
Symptoms of codependency, resources and information for partners of addicts and alcoholics, help for adult children of alcoholics and people raised in dysfunctional families.

http://www.mentalhelp.net/
Comprehensive listing of codependency information and self-help resources online.

http://www.myselfhelp.com/HomePage.html
http://www.12steps.org/
The 12Step Cyber Cafe, a place of help, hope and healing for hurting people.

http://www.therapistfinder.net/help/childhelp.html
Childhelp USA

"Child abuse kills more children in America than do accidental falls, drowning, choking on food, suffocation or fires in the home."
                    -*United States Department of Justice*

http://www.rainn.org/
The Rape, Abuse & Incest National Network (RAINN) is the nation's largest anti-sexual assault organization. RAINN operates the National Sexual Assault Hotline at 1.800.656.HOPE and carries out programs to prevent sexual assault, help victims and ensure that rapists are brought to justice. Inside, you'll find statistics, counseling resources, prevention tips, news and more.

http://www.geocities.com/WestHollywood/1769/survivor2.html#hotlines
Links to lists of hotlines

http://www.winternet.com/~webpage/adolrecovery.html
Adolescent substance abuse and recovery resources

http://www.prevent-abuse-now.com/

http://www.hopeandhealing.com/
Alcoholism—Hope and Healing web chronicles spiritual journeys and personal transformations possible for the family affected by alcoholism with extensively reviewed resources, original feature articles, daily reflections and interactive activities relating to alcoholism and codependency.

http://www.assertivehelp.com/mentalhealthresources.htm
http://open-mind.org/Abuse.htm
Information on current abuse issues, a support group, newsletter, poetry and chat for survivors of childhood abuse, their family and friends.

http://www.geocities.com/marie_w89/themightyphoenixindex.html

SUPPORT INFORMATION FOR
SURVIVORS OF SEXUAL ASSAULT

Your Body Belongs to You, by Cornelia Maude Spleman. Illustrated by Teri Weidner. Albert Whitman & Co, 2000. (This book is for parents and teachers of young children, and more focused on prevention.)

Children and Trauma: A Guide for Parents and Professionals, by Cynthia Monahan. Jossey-Bass, 1993.

How Long Does it Hurt? A Guide to Recovering from Incest and Sexual Abuse for Teenagers, Their Friends, and Their Families, by Cynthia Mather, Kristina Debye, Judy Wood and Eliana Gill. Jossey-Bass, 1994.

Handbook for Treatment of Attachment-Trauma Problems in Children, by Beverly Jack. The Free Press, 1994.

Trauma in the Lives of Children: Crisis and Stress Management Techniques for Teachers, Counselors, and Student Service Professionals, by Kendall Johnson. Hunter House, 1998.

Allies in Healing: When the Person You Love Was Sexually Abused as a Child, by Laura Davis. Perrenial Books, 1991.

Outgrowing the Pain Together: A Book for Spouses and Partners of Adults Abused as Children, by Eliana Gil. DTP, 1992.

Childhelp USA's National Child Abuse Hotline
1-800-422-4453
(1-800-4ACHILD)
Childhelp USA is a non-profit organization "dedicated to meeting the physical, emotional, educational, and spiritual needs of abused and neglected children." Its programs and services include this hotline, which children can call with complete anonymity and confidentiality. To know what to expect when you call, see How We Help

on their website. From the site: "The Childhelp USA® National Child Abuse Hotline is open 7 days a week, 24 hours a day. Don't be afraid to call. No one is silly or unimportant to us. If something is bothering you or you want information, CALL!" To learn more about reporting child abuse or neglect in your state, see Report Child Abuse.

Rape Abuse & Incest National Network
1-800-656-4673 (HOPE)
RAINN is a national network of rape crisis centers. This service links callers to the nearest center automatically. Rape crisis centers are staffed with trained volunteers and paid staff members who also have knowledge of sexual abuse issues and services (though sometimes they are not adequately prepared to refer male survivors). All calls are confidential and callers may remain anonymous if they wish.

National Domestic Violence/Abuse Hotline
1-800-799-SAFE
1-800-799-7233
1-800-787-3224 TDD
This is a twenty-four-hour-a-day hotline, staffed by trained volunteers who are ready to connect people with emergency help in their own communities, including emergency services and shelters. The staff can also provide information and referrals for a variety of non-emergency services, including counseling for adults and children and assistance in reporting abuse. They have an extensive database of domestic violence treatment providers in all US states and territories. Many staff members speak languages besides English and they have twenty-four-hour access to translators for approximately 150 languages. For the hearing impaired, there is a TDD number. This is a good resource for people who are experiencing or have experienced domestic violence or abuse, or who suspect that someone they know is being abused (though it is not perfect and may not have the best number in your area). All calls to the hotline are confidential and callers may remain anonymous if they wish.

Notes

Chapter 1

1. http://www.healthierliving.org
2. Swobe, Coe. "Career Killers: Codependency." *Nevada Lawyer*, November 2003 (adapted with permission from the National Mental Health Association and the Oregon Attorney Assistance Program).
3. http://www.codependents.org
4. http://www.recovery-man.com/coda/codependency.htm
5. Clark, Clinton S. "The Addictive Pull: Stormy Weather Ahead," from "I'm Not OK When...You're Not." 1993. http://www.artdsm.com/recover/2.html
6. http://www.allaboutcounseling.com

Chapter 5

1. Windling, Terry. "Women in Fairy Tales," (a talk given at Antigone Books, Tucson, AZ, March, 1997). http://www.endicott-studio.com/rdrm/forwnft.html
2. Gabeba Baderoon, Herman Wittenberg and Chris Roper (eds). "The Subversive Value of Feminist Fairy Tales: Overthrowing Some Grimm Stereotypes," by Jody Regel. *Inter Action 4. Proceedings of the Fourth Postgraduate Conference.* Bellville: UWC Press. 1996

Chapter 7

1. "Violence, Women and the Media," Issue Brief Series. Studio City, CA: Mediascope Press. 2000. http://www.mediascope.org/pubs/ibriefs/vwm.htm
2. St. Lawrence, J.S. and D.J. Joyner. "The Effects of Sexually Violent Rock Music on Male's Acceptance of Violence Against Women." *Psychology of Women Quarterly*, 15, 49-63. 1991.

Chapter 8

1. Oskamp, S. and M Costanzo (eds). *Gender issues in contemporary society*. Newbury Park, CA: Sage Publications, 1993.
2. "Eating Disorders 101 Guide: A Summary of Issues, Statistics and Resources." www.renfrewcenter.com/uploads/resources/1067338472_1.doc
3. "Renfrew Center Expert Says Toys Aimed at Young Girls Can Damage Self-Esteem." The Renfrew Center, via PR Newswire, January 31, 1997. http://www.kidsource.com/kidsource/content2/news2/girls_esteem.html
4. "Reflections of Girls in the Media: A Two-Part Study on Gender and Media" (April 1997). http://www.childrennow.org/media/mc97/ReflectSummary.cfm
5. "Trends in Educational Equity of Girls and Women: 2004." Figure K: Percent of bachelor's degrees conferred to females, by selected fields of study: 1969-70 and 2000-01. http://nces.ed.gov/pubs2005/equity/Section12.asp
6. "Talking to Kids About Gender Stereotypes" Tipsheets. http://www.media-awareness.ca/english/resources/tip_sheets/gender_tip.cfm

Chapter 11

1. National Clearinghouse on Child Abuse and Neglect Information. "Child Maltreatment 2002: Summary of Key Findings." 2004. http://nccanch.acf.hhs.gov/pubs/factsheets/canstats.cfm

2. "Child Abuse: Types, Signs, Symptoms, Causes and Help." http://www.helpguide.org/mental /Child_abuse_physical_emotional_sexual_neglect.htm

3. Mullen, Peter E. and Jillian Fleming. "Long-term Effects of Child Sexual Abuse." *Issues in Child Abuse Prevention*, No. 9, 1997, from the National Child Protection Clearinghouse, Australia. http://www.aifs.gov.au/nch/issues9.html

4. Hopper, Jim, Ph.D. "Sexual Abuse of Males: Prevalence, Possible Lasting Effects, and Resources." http://www.jimhopper.com/male-ab/

5. Baskerville, Stephen. "The Truth About Child Abuse," from The Center for Children's Justice, Pennsylvania Chapter. http://pfcr.childrensjustice.org/Articles/childabusetruth.htm

6. Gallagher, Maggie. *The Abolition of Marriage.* n.p.: Regnery Publishing, 1996.

7. Mullen, P. E., J.L. Martin, S.E. Anderson, S.E. Romans and Herbison, G. P. "The long-term impact of the physical, emotional, and sexual abuse of children: A community study." *Child Abuse and Neglect*, 1996, pp. 20, 7-21.

8. Moeller, T. P. and G.A. Bachmann. "The combined effects of physical, sexual, and emotional abuse during childhood: Long-term health consequences for women." *Child Abuse and Neglect*, 1993, pp. 17, 623-640.

9. Klein, I. and R.J. Bulman. "Trauma history and personal narratives: Some clues to coping among survivors of child abuse." *Child Abuse & Neglect*, 1996, pp. 20, 45-54.

10. Joubert, Joseph. "Breaking the Cycle: Children Need Models Rather than Critics." http://www.loveourchildrenusa.org/breakingthecycle